RECOVERING THE 'TRUE CHURCH'

CHALLENGES FOR
AUSTRALIAN CATHOLICISM BEYOND
THE PLENARY COUNCIL

RECOVERING THE 'TRUE CHURCH'

PAUL COLLINS

COVENTRY
PRESS

Published in Australia by
Coventry Press
33 Scoresby Road
Bayswater VIC 3153

ISBN 9781922589163

Copyright © Paul Collins 2022

All rights reserved. Other than for the purposes and subject to the conditions prescribed under the *Copyright Act*, no part of this publication may be reproduced, stored in a retrieval system, or transmitted in any form or by any means, electronic, mechanical, photocopying, recording or otherwise, without the prior permission of the publisher.

Scripture quotations are from the *New Revised Standard Version Bible*, copyright 1989, Division of Christian Education of the National Council of the Churches of Christ in the United States of America. Used by permission. All rights reserved.

Catalogue-in-Publication entry is available from the National Library of Australia, http://catalogue.nla.gov.au

Cover design by Ian James – www.jgd.com.au
Text design by Coventry Press
Set in Gentium

Printed in Australia

Contents

Acknowledgments 6
Abbreviations 8

Part 1   A Context for the Plenary 9

    Chapter One: Recovering the 'True Church' 11
    Chapter Two: The Real Church 21
    Chapter Three: Models of Church 42
    Chapter Four: The Secular World 58
    Chapter Five: Proclaiming the Gospel in Australia .. 76

Part 2   The Actual Plenary 93

    Chapter Six: The Plenary Council 95
    Endnotes 126
    Bibliography 130
    Index 133

Acknowledgments

Writers are dependent on many people; many are acknowledged in the endnotes. But there are several people I want to thank personally. Dr Peter Wilkinson's research has long been a tower of strength for the renewal movement and he has also been able to guide the actual proceedings of the Plenary Council with his wisdom and knowledge. He has certainly helped me on many occasions, generously and spontaneously. Another Peter who has worked tirelessly for renewal is Peter Johnstone who has led the Australasian Catholic Coalition for Church Reform with great commitment.

Others whose wisdom and guidance I've drawn upon are Emeritus Professor John Warhurst, Chair of Concerned Catholics Canberra-Goulburn. John's leadership of CCCG has been inspiring and his participation in and commentary on the Plenary has been very important. Francis Sullivan, Chair of Catholic Social Services Australia and the former CEO of the Truth, Justice and Healing Council, is a true leader of the Australian church and again I owe much to his insight and experience. I quote both John and Francis often in the book. Francis' wife, Susan Sullivan, is another who has written wisely and insightfully about both ministry and tradition.

Hugh McGinlay at Coventry Press made many wise suggestions and has been an enthusiastic and supportive editor. Thanks, Hugh, and to all at Coventry.

Acknowledgments

My final word of thanks is to my wife, Marilyn Hatton, who read the entire manuscript several times and who made many helpful comments, especially about the ordering of the book. Even more, she has always been there for me.

Abbreviations

ACBC	Australian Catholic Bishops Conference
ACCCR	Australasian Catholic Coalition for Church Reform
CCCG	Concerned Catholic Canberra-Goulburn
CFR	Catholics for Renewal
CSO	Catholics Speak Out (formerly Catholics for Ministry)
LG	*Lumen Gentium* (Vatican II)
LSCR	Light from the Southern Cross
PC	Plenary Council
RC	Royal Commission into Institutional Responses to Child Sexual Abuse
WATAC	Women and the Australian Church

Part 1
A Context for the Plenary

Chapter One

Recovering the 'True Church'

One True Church

In the old pre-Vatican II days, we used to talk about 'the one, true church', implying that all other churches, let alone the other great religions, were 'false' and that you had to get with the Catholic strength if you wanted an assurance that you were following Jesus and, more importantly, were saved. It was, of course, a form of Catholic triumphalism that now seems like gobsmacking arrogance and was really a hangover from the monarchical church of the seventeenth century. This book is entitled 'recovering the true church', by which I mean finding our way back beyond the triumphalist church to the larger, genuine Catholic tradition. The 'true Church' here is the one that proclaims 'the glory of God shining in the face of Jesus Christ' (2 Corinthians 4:6), the community that is grounded in the gospel and proclaims the Catholic tradition 'whether the time is favourable or unfavourable' (2 Timothy, 4:2), 'in season and out of season', as some translate it.

I use the word 'recover' purposely because right now we are in a period of far-reaching transition and we're going to have to be clear-headed to remain faithful to genuine Catholicism. The contemporary church has lost its ability to speak meaningfully of Jesus, the gospel and the genuine tradition; already 90%

or more of self-identified Australian Catholics have withdrawn from faith practice. And this is happening right across the developed world. The church has already 'lost the working class and has great difficulty approaching young people today', Bishop Georg Bätzing, President of the German Bishops' Conference says. He warns that it is now in danger of losing women: 'Their departure is imminent as they feel they are being left out'.[1]

The same is true in Australia. The church is publicly identified as an abusive, secretive institution, obsessed with sex and gender issues, closely linked to our culpable failure to protect vulnerable children in our communities. The result: Catholicism is largely ignored, even despised by our fellow citizens. The Plenary Council (PC) is the attempt of the bishops to confront these issues.

If there is one thing the PC has already demonstrated, it is that there is still a lot of passionate engagement with Catholicism among the Australian faithful. The 222,000 people who participated in the preliminary consultations and the 17,457 written submissions sent to the Plenary organisers showed that. Sure, the majority are of a certain age, but given all the vicissitudes they've been through since the close of Vatican II in 1965, it is extraordinary that people are still so committed. The seething energy of the renewal movement is there for everyone to see. It is sad that so few of the bishops show an equivalent level of passion or commitment. What these faithful people want to recover is the 'true Church', by which they mean the Vatican II model of the pilgrim people of God.

To do this they will have to get behind and beyond the model of church that dominates at the present moment. This is what we generally call the 'monarchical' model. This entered the tradition during the post-Reformation period and the seventeenth century. It was given shape and form by the theologian Saint Robert Bellarmine in his massive three volume *Controversies* against the Protestants (1593). Bellarmine (1542-1621), Galileo's nemesis, claimed that the pope was essentially the 'divinely instituted' monarch of the church and that even decrees of ecumenical councils needed papal confirmation to be binding. He says unequivocally: 'The church of Christ is a most perfect kingdom and an absolute monarchy which neither depends on the people, nor has from its origin, but depends on the divine will alone'.[2] The pope, Bellarmine said, cannot be judged, deposed, or punished by anyone, including a council. He is supreme judge in deciding on faith and morals; what he teaches is, *ipso facto*, by that very fact, infallible. The Bellarmine vision was enshrined at the First Vatican Council in 1870. Later, I will discuss changing models of the church, but here it is sufficient to say that we are largely operating out of a model whose roots are found in the 16th and 17th centuries.

But the Catholic tradition is much richer than this. Behind Bellarmine is a wealth of ecclesiology, or what the church is and how it operates. 'Tradition' is the key word here, but it's a problematic word in contemporary English. It usually refers to hanging onto the past, a harking back to an idealised nirvana. The word tradition is derived from the Latin verb *trado* meaning to hand over, to pass on, or transmit. There is an active element here. It is not just a matter of passively receiving what was handed down, but creatively developing it in the process of receiving it, living it and handing it on to succeeding generations. This is an active notion that places us in dynamic but critical continuity with the past, a living interaction with the present, and the creative ability to imagine the future.

Tradition is not just a harking back to the past. That's one element. The other is that in the very process of handing on the tradition, we create it anew. The theologian who understood this best was Saint John Henry Newman. At the heart of his theology is the act of embracing change while rooted in continuity with the past. His theology stands beyond the utterly false dichotomy of the so-called 'hermeneutics of continuity and rupture', a caricature of the post-Vatican II period promoted by Benedict XVI.[3] This pope argued that, for some, Vatican II was a 'rupture', a discontinuity, that is the council completely broke with the past almost creating the church anew. Whereas the 'continuity' brigade, to which Benedict, of course, belonged, believed Vatican II had both maintained and developed the on-going Catholic tradition. This dichotomy is completely artificial, a caricature. No sensible Catholic thinks the Council was a complete break with the past, a completely new beginning in which you can make things up to suit yourself.

Newman, in contrast, argues that the more the church grows, develops and changes, the more it truly becomes itself. Using the metaphor of a river, he says: 'It is indeed sometimes said that the stream is clearest near the spring. Whatever use may be fairly made of this image, it does not apply to the history of a philosophy or belief [or church], which on the contrary is more equable, and purer, and stronger, when its bed has become deep, and broad... Here below to live is to change, and to be perfect is to have changed often'. I have omitted part of the passage where he says some extraordinarily pertinent things for the contemporary church. For instance, he assures us that 'vital elements' of the church need 'disengaging from what is foreign and temporary', and that 'from time to time [the church] makes essays which fail, and are in consequence abandoned. It seems in suspense which way to go; it wavers, and at length strikes out in one definite direction'. This seems very much like our situation today as we waver in our attempt to discover the way forward. Finally, he reassures us that the church changes, 'in order to remain the same'. Newman says the vital elements are there just waiting for us to rediscover them as we 'disengage from what is foreign and temporary'. We need not worry, because sometimes the church 'makes essays which fail and are... abandoned'.[4] The monarchical church is one of these. It made sense in its time, but that time passed with the French Revolution and the emergence of the modern world. We should not be fooling ourselves that we can integrate the contemporary pilgrim people of God into a monarchy. God's Spirit is still there leading us onward.

Recovering the True Church arose from a shift in my own thinking about Catholicism. For years, I was convinced that the central issue for those who embraced Vatican II was the integration of the Council's renewed ecclesiology into present church governance and structures. I often said that the primal mistake that the renewal movement made in the immediate post-council period was to wait until everyone – even the most recalcitrant – understood the conciliar challenge and was on board. While we waited, the conservatives made sure nothing changed structurally, so that the monarchical/Vatican I governance model remained intact and dominant. As a result, the PC is still struggling to deal with what are conflicting models of church.

However, we are now in the post-post-Vatican II stage after John Paul II and Benedict XVI's 'reform of the reform' has succeeded in stopping renewal in its tracks, and there is a distinct danger of us losing the New Testament-early church-Vatican II vision altogether. Precious few younger Catholics have integrated it, despite the very best efforts of Catholic educators.

I think the challenge now is to move beyond the outdated monarchical ecclesiology altogether and begin to sketch out and live a renewed people of God model of church. This model is

New Testament focused, engaged with the world around us, and committed to proclaiming the spiritual and human fulfilment that a relationship with God in Christ brings. The game has not only changed, but we're now really playing in a different league altogether. I'm not saying we abandon the bishops, even though most of them are not listening. They will re-join us when we evolve a working model of church that God's Spirit inspires.

What to do?

Not everyone in the renewal movement agrees with me here. A significant number of people I've spoken to emphasised that now is not the time to withdraw from engagement with the institutional church and bishops, especially given the energy that we've already put into the PC process. Remain in the game and 'keep the bastards honest', especially by holding 'the hierarchy to account for the implementation of the Royal Commission's recommendations'.[5] Not that these people don't think we should envisage a future vision. What they are saying is that we can play both games, both the bishops' and our own. But the problem for me is: with so much energy being put into the PC, will the Vatican II generation have the energy and, more importantly, the time to tackle the challenge of recovering the true church?

The fact is that some renewal groups have already begun the task of building God's kingdom. This is an untidy, non-linear process that is going to have to be built from the bottom up by communities of believers. These communities pray and celebrate liturgy together, but are also outward-looking, intimately involved in ministry. Their leadership will emerge organically from the community, as happened in the early church. Many contemporary Australian renewal movements are strategically well-placed to begin to operate as these new communities; a couple of them are already well along the way to realising this, but I'd be the first to admit that it feels risky, ill-defined and it will certainly demand much harder work than just challenging bishops. Often it is women's groups who are well ahead with this.

To achieve this kind of functioning, renewal groups would build themselves up as communities through celebrating liturgy, prayer and biblical reflection together. From that foundation, they go out to ministry. They are not discussion, let alone self-help groups. They exist to serve by living-out the basic meaning of the word 'liturgy'. The word is derived from the Greek λειτουργία ('leitourgia') which basically means 'public service', or 'work for the common good'. But it also refers to the service of God – what we once called 'divine service'. Worship and ministry are intimately linked; you can't have one without the other. The ministry of these groups would be structured around the gifts of each member. The challenge is to build-up the church on the basis of the guarantees set-out in the Letter to the Ephesians: 'You are no longer strangers and aliens, but you are citizens with the saints and members of the household of God, built upon the foundation of the apostles and prophets, with Christ himself as the cornerstone' (2:29). As citizens and members of God's household, the Spirit has given each one 'gifts' so that 'some would be apostles, some prophets, some evangelists, some pastors and teachers, to equip the saints for the work of ministry for building up the body of Christ' (4:11). Also, if groups are focused on ministry to the community rather than all sorts of special interest 'causes', it's less likely they'll take stances that lead to conflict with other Catholics.

The one caveat I'd mention here is that liturgical composition is not a free-for-all, or an instrument for the expression of pet peeves. You don't make up the liturgy as you go along. True liturgy has a form that is almost symphonic in its structure. Thus, some people in the community need to be trained in liturgical composition. Liturgical form was something the church recognised from early on as they perceived that liturgical composition is a gift from the Spirit that wasn't given to all. We can see the form of the early liturgy in the *Apostolic Tradition* of the anti-pope Hippolytus of Rome (170-235), which describes contemporary eucharistic and baptismal liturgies used by the Roman church.

Talking about already established communities, I received a response from Women's Wisdom in the Church (WWitch) group which pointed out that for many women an 'alternative way of Church is already a reality, as we meet in groups to pray, meditate, consider feminist theology and develop and implement liturgies. And we have been ministering to our friends, group members and fellow parishioners for as long as most of us can remember'. WWitch favours a both/and approach. 'The only way we can do this', they say, 'is to be true to the call of the Spirit within our lives while still communicating with the bishops, no matter how implacable they are. This is the way women tend to work and... this is the best way to bring the church forward.'[6]

Some fear that the danger of schism lurks in the approach I suggest. The *Oxford Dictionary of the Christian Church* defines schism as 'formal and wilful separation from the unity of the church'. The word is derived from the Greek word σχίσμα ("schisma") from the verb meaning to tear apart or split. The *Dictionary* distinguishes schism from heresy, saying that schism is not primarily doctrinal. 'Whereas heresy is opposed to faith, schism is opposed to charity.'[7] I am certainly not recommending 'formal and wilful separation from the church', let alone a lack of charity, but a recovery of the 'true church'. The unity of the church is absolutely important and we have to discover the fine line between toxic criticism and that which 'builds up the body of Christ' (Ephesians 4:12). No one in the renewal movement wants schism. In fact, it may well be those who resist change are the ones who are in schism. If there is any suggestion of schism about our present circumstances, it seems to me that it is some of the bishops who separate themselves, and those who reject the mainstream faithful are the ones who are in borderline schism.

To conclude, I return to my primary argument: where the baptised faithful are, there is the church. What I'm arguing is that the New Testament, especially in the Pauline writings, which underpinned the theology of Vatican II, seeks to emphasise the priority of baptism and the gifts of the Spirit that come with it, creating 'a chosen people, a royal priesthood, a holy nation, a people belonging to God, that you may declare the praises of him who called you out of darkness into his wonderful light' (1 Peter 2:9-12). Emphasis is centrally important in theology and what we are trying to do in the renewal movement is to shift the focus away from the post-Reformation, monarchical, papo-centric church of Bellarmine and the First Vatican Council, to the Vatican II emphasis on the laity who constitute the vast majority of the faithful. We need to embrace an emphasis on the people of God rather than the hierarchical church. It's where you place your emphasis that really matters.

Those working for the recovery of the true church are the ones who will build the bridge between Vatican II and the future. Many Australian Catholics are already doing that. But they'll have to be content that they won't see the result of their efforts in their own lifetimes. At most they can only guess what the church of the future will look like.

It's a frustrating place to be, but there you are!

Chapter Two

The Real Church

'Business as usual'

On December 5, 2019 in his *Prison Journal*, Cardinal George Pell commented that 'the potential for strife and further damage [to the church] is real with the [2021-2022] Plenary Council'.[8] He need not have worried; as it turned out, the PC appears to have been a masterclass in business-as-usual as it side-stepped the real issues facing Australian Catholicism. Certainly, there were people inside the gathering who tried very hard to focus the discussion on the questions that had emerged in the nationwide, year-long consultation process and the 17,457 written submissions that had been sent to the Plenary organisers. But those who managed the process – either consciously or otherwise – kept the proceedings well away from 'unsafe' issues, like ordination, particularly of women, gender, governance and episcopal power. What I want to do in this book is to confront the issues the PC side-stepped and to develop a wider theological and sociological context that takes seriously the concerns raised by the consultation process.

The most important and basic of these was the need to look outward, beyond the borders of the church, to the broader community in which Catholicism operates. While there were scattered references to Australian society in the PC, there was no coherent, systematic reflection on Australian culture. The PC completely side-stepped the call of Vatican Council II in the Constitution on the Church in the Modern World (*Gaudium et Spes*) to 'recognise and understand the world in which we live, its explanations, its longings, and its often-dramatic characteristics'. The Council called us to scrutinise the signs of the times and interpret them in the light of the gospel. It's only then that faith can respond to the culture's questionings 'in language intelligible to each generation' (Paragraph 4).

Put another way: while the gospel offers a critique of culture, you can't communicate that criticism if you can't talk to the culture, or don't understand it, or reject it. That's what happens when you incestuously look inward, turning Catholicism into a semi-sect, which is a real temptation for people who favour a narrow, defensive orthodoxy in responding to the world. They tend to project blame outward onto constructed caricatures of atheism and intolerant secularism. This is not to say that there isn't a corrosive anti-religious strain in modern secularism, but it is to say that we need to get our own house in order before we begin projecting blame outward.

The reality is that a retreat into sectarianism is incompatible with genuine Catholicism. It is the antithesis of the kind of Vatican II openness to the world, tolerant acceptance of others and a sense of religious pluralism that most thinking believers have been formed in and embraced. At the core of being Catholic is 'catholicity'. The word 'catholic' is derived from the Greek word καθολικός ('katholikos') from a preposition meaning 'according to' and a noun meaning 'whole'. The *Shorter Oxford Dictionary* defines 'catholic' as 'the quality of having sympathies with or being all-embracing; broad-mindedness; tolerance'. The derivation of the word implies an open, embracing, wholistic community that accepts people as they are. James Joyce was right when in *Finnegan's Wake* he described Catholicism as 'Here comes everybody'.

Explaining catholicity's theological basis, American theologian, Avery Dulles, SJ, says that catholicity has four traits which he characterises as breadth, length, depth, and height.[9] First, breadth or inclusiveness, which means an openness to various cultures and opposition to sectarianism and religious individualism; second, the 2000 year-length of church history that bridges succeeding generations and periods as it hands on the catholic tradition; third, a depth and universality that is open to truth and value wherever it exists in the world; finally, a looking toward the Holy Spirit whose indwelling creates the unity of the church through which we participate in the life of God. To be genuinely catholic, the church must include these four characteristics which are deeply embedded in church history and were given modern expression in the vision of the church articulated at Vatican II. Here the church is defined as the living sacrament of God's presence and the place where God's sovereignty is acknowledged and expressed through a participative community of people dedicated to the service of the world and characterised by collegiality and ecumenism.

For sure, there has always been a tension between a broad, open vision of Catholicism rooted in living experience, and a static, sectarian view of faith; it runs right through church history. A modern manifestation of the narrower vision is the revival of what's called 'remnant theology'. In the Hebrew scriptures the remnant are the Israelites who survive after the Babylonian conquest and exile in 597BC. The prophet Isaiah (10:22) says that although the people of Israel were 'like the sand of the sea', only a remnant of them will return to the homeland. In the New Testament, Paul says that the church itself is 'a remnant, chosen by grace' (Romans 11:5). This remnant theme recurs whenever believers seeking purity and separation from the world retreat into sects of various sorts; many of the most extreme are described in Ronald Knox's fascinating book *Enthusiasm*.[10]

A recent re-appearance of the remnant notion came with Benedict XIV's idea that the contemporary church will increasingly become a minority of committed believers in a predominately secular society. He believed that 'camp follower', cultural Catholics will drop away, leaving only 'a little flock' (Luke 12:32) that is prepared to proclaim the kingdom of God in the struggle against personal and social evil. This is perhaps an understandable Eurocentric response to the precipitous decline of Christianity in the Western world, including Australia, since the 1960s. It may well be that Benedict is right and that the future lies with creative minorities, but certainly not with hyper-orthodox, sectarian in-groups focused on intramural issues like the Latin Mass.

Australian Catholicism

What we're concerned about here is the future of mainstream Catholicism in Australia and, more broadly, the future of Christianity. There is no doubt that Christianity generally and Catholicism specifically are very much on the defensive nowadays. In the case of Catholicism, the reason is obvious: the sexual abuse crisis. Catholicism's reputation has been effectively trashed in the media and wider community by this crisis and church leaders' appalling, long-term failure to deal decisively with clerical criminals. The revelations of the Royal Commission into Institutional Responses to Sexual Abuse (RC) reinforced the church's toxic reputation.

Yet, despite this, Catholicism is still enormously influential in Australia. In the 2016 census, 22.6% of the population, that is 5,291,834 people, self-reported as Catholic. The church employs more than 230,000 people, making it close to the biggest private employer in the country with more people than Wesfarmers, or all the major banks combined. It's a serious player in the educational, health, aged care and social service sectors. Since the 1830s and for much of Australian history, it was the Catholic and other Christian churches that provided the lion's share of these services. After the 1860s, with the establishment of state schools, government aid was entirely withdrawn from church schools, although support for services to the poor and sick was maintained on a dollar-for-dollar basis.

Nowadays, government supports the churches' social welfare ministry on a contractual basis, with Catholicism maintaining some fifty-two organisations across a range of service provisions: homelessness, refugees, drug, alcohol, gambling, family violence, foster care, disability, counselling, overseas aid and employment. In 2016, the lay-run Saint Vincent de Paul Society had 20,736 members and 41,152 volunteers, making it the largest voluntary charity in the country, providing an enormous range of services. In 2021, Catholic schools were educating some 777,000 students in 1746 primary and secondary schools, or 19.4% of all enrolments. It provides almost a quarter of health and aged care.[11] The striking thing about this is that since the 1960s church and state have worked closely together in the provision of services across all these sectors, with the government providing about 70% of funding for all the church's ministries, except parishes and dioceses. This relationship is unique, with no real parallel anywhere in the world.

But the heart of the Catholic crisis is that this vast ministerial superstructure is based on increasingly weak ecclesial foundations.

The simple fact is that the number of committed Catholics who do the bulk of the church's work is contracting at an increasing rate. You see this in terms of affiliation with the church. A broadly nominal, cultural affiliation, as reflected in the number of self-identifying Catholics in the census, is falling. From a high in 1996 when Catholics made up 27% of the population, this dropped to 25.3% in 2011 and to 22.6% in 2016, a fall of 4.4% in twenty years. There's little doubt that there will be a further decrease in Catholic affiliation in the 2021 Census.

Conservative Catholics usually blame this on Vatican II and its aftermath. This is a mistaken interpretation; in fact, the opposite is true. The world changed in the 1960s with a tectonic shift occurring that involved a radical change in the role and status of women with the advent of feminism, the ascendancy of science and technology, and a new understanding of sexuality spurring the widespread acceptance of gender diversity and fluidity. Vatican II, particularly in *Gaudium et Spes*, opened-up Catholicism to this emerging world and laid the foundation for a creative and critical interaction with it. The church's leadership has abjectly failed to apply this opening-up creatively and critically to these cultural shifts and this has had an inevitable impact on the church's credibility among Catholics and the community generally.

In the post-Vatican II period, there was a catastrophic failure in leadership. Pope Paul VI only half-heartedly introduced the Vatican II reforms. This was intensified by John Paul II, who introduced an agenda that reflected his Polish, idiosyncratic and narrow vision of Catholicism. His twenty-seven-year papacy (1978-2005), followed by that of Benedict XVI (2005-2013) were disastrous, alienating many Catholics, particularly in the Western world. The bishops appointed by these popes reflected papal agendas and local Catholics increasingly felt leaderless and bereft as the church lost many of its lay and priestly leadership cadre, the kind of emotionally intelligent people essential for it to move into the future. Many good, pastoral priests left the ministry because they felt unable to implement Vatican II, some of them to marry, while frustrated lay leaders severed affiliation or drifted away. Also, many post-Vatican II priests remained in ministry despite the frustrations and they are still generously serving the church community as stalwarts of renewed Catholicism, many of them now well beyond retirement age.

The bishop 'problem'

At the heart of the church's problem is the role of bishops. The present reality is that 'the bishops' credibility is shot to pieces', as ACBC president Coleridge admitted. He bluntly told media in Rome in February 2019 that if you did a word association test and you said the words 'Catholic church', most Australians would answer 'abuse' and would 'associate "Catholic priest" with "paedophile" and "Catholic bishop" with worse than [a] paedophile, a "liar or cover-upper, untrustworthy"'.[12] If the ACBC president is willing to admit that to overseas journalists, it's not surprising to learn that most Australian Catholics have little confidence in the bishops, with a few exceptions. What is clear is that a substantial number of bishops are not really committed to the PC and are determined to maintain the status quo.

The essential problem is that many bishops see any attempt to demand accountability and transparency as a threat to their authority, which they think of as derived from their ordination. In one sense, they feel a responsibility to maintain the structure of the church as they received it; in their understanding of their role, they feel they don't have room to move on what they perceive as the essentials of the faith because episcopal ordination makes them teachers and shepherds of the flock. For them, any questioning of the present form of church governance or of their power and authority is throwing doubt on a divinely ordained church structure and they have identified themselves personally with their office. This reflects a lack of emotional intelligence and immaturity as they derive their personal worth from their clerical identification with their role.

But there's another, more blatantly political side to the appointment of Australian bishops. Since 1990, George Pell has been influential in Rome. That was the year in which he was appointed a member of the Congregation for the Doctrine of the Faith, the Church's doctrinal watchdog, then headed by Joseph Ratzinger, later Benedict XVI. But perhaps even more important was Pell's appointment to the Congregation for Bishops which appoints bishops worldwide. This gave him the inside running on Australian nominations. As Father Eric Hodgens notes, both these Vatican jobs 'involved regular participation in Roman meetings and wheeling and dealing in Vatican politics'. Through his influence, particularly at the Bishops' Congregation, Pell has made sure that 'no episcopal appointment for the last two and more decades [in Australia] has been made without his active promotion or passive permission'.[13] This influence has been maintained through his friendship with the French-Canadian, Cardinal Marc Ouellet, Prefect of the Congregation for Bishops.

The direct result is that only bishops who generally share Pell's approach to Catholicism are appointed. Pell told the Eternal Word TV network in 2021 that bishops should 'speak-up on issues where you know you're not going to get the popular vote, where you know most of the people are against you.

Basically, [bishops] have an obligation to keep presenting the teachings of Christ and the teachings of the Catholic Church'.[14] The problem here is working out exactly what Pell means by the teachings of Christ and the church. His theological definitions are narrow, literalist, some might say 'fundamentalist'. Answering a question from RC counsel, Gail Furness, about the church's failure to address sexual abuse and the 'structural problems in the way in which the church operates', Pell claimed that this failure doesn't 'call into question the divine structure of the church, which goes back to the New Testament [including]... the role of the pope and bishops'. The church's problems, he says, 'have overwhelmingly been more personal faults, personal failures, rather than structures'.[15] Here we get to the nub of his understanding of the church; for him the structure is part of the 'divine plan', so rooted in the New Testament that it cannot be changed; it's immutable.

His views represent a narrow orthodoxy and his understanding of the church is absolutist and authoritarian. Therefore, it's understandable that he would make sure that only priests who shared his views, or men he could manage, would be promoted to the episcopate. That's not to say that all the Australian bishops are Pell appointees, or in the Pell mould. But there is no doubt that he still has a strong hold on several of the senior archbishops and a number of local bishops. The result: a sizeable minority of bishops who share Pell's approach are not overly enthusiastic about the PC and are determined to keep it under control.

Writing recently about the US bishops, theologian Daniel P. Horan makes the comment that many of them don't read widely, engage in robust conversation and dialogue, or learn from perspectives, sources and cultures different to their own. He notes an anti-intellectual streak amongst them leading to an 'arrogance that has led so many bishops to feel they are entitled to make sweeping judgments [that] can... be traced back to a misplaced sense of unassailable knowledge or certitude, which belongs to absolutely no individual minister, including the pope himself'.[16] You can see something similar among the Australian bishops. They live sheltered lives, divorced from the reality of close relationship, marriage and family, struggle and survival in the real world. There is a significant lack of curiosity; they only read material that they agree with; when they have to face media, they tend to pontificate and lack an ability to engage with opinions different to their own. I think that this kind of sheltered certitude goes a long way to explaining how they insulate themselves even from active and committed Catholics.

Pope Francis has lessened Rome's centralised, smothering grip on the local churches and encouraged initiative. He has asked bishops to get beyond their inertia and involve themselves in synodal-consultative processes, but apparently lacking leadership skills, risk-averse bishops seem loathe or unable to assume responsibility for their local churches. The Australian bishops are past masters at claiming that even minor decisions are 'beyond their competence', or 'inappropriate at this time'. An example of this is the bishops' failure to take the initiative in 2017 when Pope Francis said he was open to the idea of ordaining married men who could potentially help the priest shortage. 'We must think about whether *viri probati* are a possibility', he said, referring to mature married men who were already experienced in ministry and had the requisite qualifications. 'Then', he added, 'we have to decide what tasks they can take on, for example in remote communities.' He was not advocating optional celibacy.[17]

This was an opening for local church leadership to take the initiative and petition Rome to allow ordination of married men. To their credit, a couple of Australian bishops expressed their support for this, but the ACBC maintained a stolid silence. They probably felt justified when Francis, possibly not wanting to contradict openly the retired-Benedict XVI, seemingly backed-away from the *viri probati* proposal at the time of the Synod for Amazonia in early 2020. But the reality is that locally-born *viri probati* could enormously assist Australia's ministerial crisis.

Here the church is already very short of priests and this is impacting in urban and especially rural parishes. Bishops are dealing with it by closing parishes, combining them, or establishing so-called 'pastoral regions'. Most dioceses are also dealing with the priest short-fall by importing foreign priests, who in 2021 already constituted 55% of all priests in parishes. This is no solution and it is asset-stripping the source countries of clergy. Father James Clarke, President of the National Council of Priests, warned in 2018 that the importation of foreign priests into Australia on temporary, three- to five-year Sub-Class 457 Visas, was a stop gap policy that 'was a doomed experiment which admittedly had some modest success, but overall has failed dismally'.[18] David Timbs has pointed out that many overseas priests lacked 'critically important skills' for ministry in Australia, including experience in working with and treating women equally, and in some cases had 'inflated expectations of clerical privilege and entitlement' that made it 'near impossible' for them to interact with a laity brought-up in a strong democratic tradition.[19]

Sexual abuse crisis

The most toxic issue facing the Australian church is child sexual abuse. The recent RC revealed a pervasive element of criminality and cover-up that has utterly disfigured Catholicism. It has also exposed appalling mistreatment of innocent children and their families not only by priest perpetrators, but also by church authorities who attempted to sweep these crimes aside to save the reputation and assets of the church. The results have been horrendous and the truth is out there now for all to see. Former chair of the bishops' Truth, Justice and Healing Council, Francis Sullivan says that 'There is now a deep malaise compounded by a simmering anger within the community about the church and child sexual abuse... The very fact that the church was on trial rips at the heart of what the church is meant to be... [There has been] a profound loss of direction, integrity, purpose and meaning at the heart of the church. A spiritual wasteland... People say the church now needs to get its house back in order but, I say we have to re-build the house'.[20] That's exactly right. Professor Patrick Parkinson points out that 'the levels of abuse in the Catholic Church are strikingly out of proportion with any other church – and... this is an international pattern'.[21] We're now seeing child abuse in many local churches beyond the English-speaking world in Germany, Chile, France, Italy, Poland and elsewhere.

Why is clerical child abuse so prevalent in the Catholic church? An insightful study of priest abusers was carried-out by the Irish psychologist, Dr Marie Keenan, of University College Dublin.[22] Her evidence to the Australian RC in February 2017 helps our understanding of the psychological dynamics of clerical perpetrators, and also the 'theological' context that nurtured their abuse.

She speaks of it in terms of 'the interplay of power and powerlessness', commenting that her research shows that 'the structural contradictions of [abusive priests'] clerical lives kept them inherently powerless, while at the same time set them above other non-ordained or non-vowed men and women. While formation and the structure of clerical life kept them sexually and relationally immature, ordination and sacred consecration set them apart as elite, superior to others'. Essentially, their seminary formation and the presuppositions underlying their concept of priesthood told them that they were superior to the ordinary people to whom they ministered because they were 'ontologically changed' as priests or, for non-ordained brothers, their vows as religious made them 'sacred' because God had specially called them. 'Influenced by this theology', Keenan says, 'it is little wonder that priesthood was construed by clergy and laity alike as a personal gift and a permanent sacred calling, rather than a gift of service to the community. It is also little wonder that a corrosive culture of clericalism was to be borne from such a theology, which was to effect clergy and laity alike'. Keenan says she is convinced that this theology of 'ontological change... set otherwise healthy men... apart from ordinary [people] in an unhealthy manner, but [it] also bred a culture of clericalism that has been part of the sexual abuse crisis in the Catholic Church'.

John Paul II highlighted this kind of theology when in 1999 he told a group of priests that they were 'ontologically configured to Christ the Priest... which is why we can say... that every priest is *'alter Christus'*.[23] The term 'ontologically configured' means that the priest in his personal essence, in the core of his being, actually becomes Christ. It implies that the ordained go beyond the ordinary baptised Christian to become a kind of 'super-Christian'. It is this idealised notion of the priesthood which blocked John Paul from recognising the depth and perniciousness of priestly sexual abuse. He simply couldn't conceive how priests completely configured to Christ could behave in such a manner. Picking up on this theme, Keenan in her evidence to the RC referred to a 2008 book by Hobart Archbishop Julian Porteous promoting this: 'A man once ordained is ontologically changed', Porteous says. 'He is a priest. Something mysterious happens'.[24] Porteous is the former rector of the Good Shepherd Seminary in Sydney.

Here it's worth noting that Jesus was a layperson; he wasn't trained formally as a rabbi, nor did he belong to the priestly caste, nor was he a scribe; it was precisely his teaching as a *layman* that infuriated the Jewish religious authorities. The notion of ritualised priesthood was only projected onto Christ in the Letter to the Hebrews, a product of the Jewish-Christian community.

The concept of ontological change is the primary source of the clerical priesthood's problems as immature men derive their sense of self-worth from an imagined exalted status above ordinary Christians. Simultaneously, their psycho-sexual development is fixated at adolescence and they fail to perceive it as completely inappropriate to form imagined equal 'friendships' with young male adolescents. 'At the level of the sexual and the emotional', Keenan says, 'their narratives paradoxically indicate that they saw children and young people as potential "friends" and "equals"'.[25] It's hard to get your head around this, except to say that these priests' sexual maturation was fixated at an adolescent level.

Another element in this perverse world is the clerical cult of secrecy which has been a characteristic of clericalism for centuries. Part of it is derived from Mediterranean culture which values reputation more than reality and which links into the notion of 'the good name of the church'. But it's clericalism that encourages a cult of secrecy. Two recent examples of disgraced cardinals stand out: Keith O'Brien of St Andrews and Edinburgh carried on an active sex life with young priests and seminarians and Theodore McCarrick of Washington abused both young adults and boys for years with impunity. How did they do it? As the *National Catholic Reporter* said: 'Cronyism and secrecy are... part of any large "hierarchy". When rumours about McCarrick and O'Brien surfaced, they were protected by... the old boys' club. They were also protected by a habit and practice of secrecy... The Catholic clerical world is the deepest and darkest closet there is'.[26] Here almost everything is done secretly. 'Accountability' and 'transparency' are meaningless words in the ecclesiastical lexicon.

All of this is re-enforced by Catholicism's (and Christianity's) long negative history regarding sexuality. Derived from other-worldly, body-denying, pre-Christian, neo-platonic philosophy, the attitude that the flesh was hopelessly compromised and all sexual expression, except in marriage, was sinful became rooted in the Western tradition through Saint Augustine (354-430AD) and his neo-platonic theology. It needs to be emphasised that the source of this was not the Bible, nor the words of Jesus, nor the New Testament, but Plato (427-347BC) as mediated by Plotinus (205-270AD), neither of whom were Christians. Their body-denying, sexually-repressive, idealised thought has become more normative in Christianity than Scripture. It was through Augustine that Western theology became infected with the notion that all sexual activity outside of marriage – the purpose of which must be procreative – was sinful.

A kind of neo-Augustinism can be found in John Paul II's so-called 'theology of the body' wherein any form of non-marital sexual activity, or even sexuality within marriage using contraceptives, is non-personalist and therefore 'utilitarian', by which he means using another person without commitment, thus rendering it sinful. He also describes sexuality outside of marriage, as well as the use of contraceptives, as 'consumerist', an eccentric use of the word in English. By this he means the use of another person without commitment.

As I pointed out in 1986 in the book *Mixed Blessings*, John Paul sees intercourse as a paradigm for the role of women.[27] In his book *Love and Responsibility*, published in Polish in 1960, he says: 'It is in the very nature of the [sexual] act that the man plays the active role and takes the initiative, while the woman is a comparatively passive partner whose function is to accept and experience'. He adds that it is enough for the woman 'to be passive and unresisting so much so that it can even take place without her volition... for instance when she is asleep or unconscious'.[28] It is statements like this that led John Paul's close friend and confidant, Dr Anna-Teresa Tymieniecka, to say of *Love and Responsibility*: 'I was truly astonished... he obviously doesn't know what he's talking about... He doesn't have experiences of that sort... He is sexually innocent'.[29] Exactly! Despite John Paul's attempt to express this inadequate theological tradition in modern 'personalist' jargon, nowadays most Catholics, particularly young Catholics, largely ignore church teaching on sexuality because they find it literally unbelievable.

Intimately connected to neo-platonic attitudes to the flesh and sexuality is the exaltation of virginity over marriage. This also lies at the root of the celibacy requirement for priests which, despite its origin in fourth-century monasticism, only became universally binding on the Western clergy when Pope Gregory VII forbade priestly marriage in March 1074 at the Synod of Rome as part of a campaign to break lay control of church property. The result: celibacy became a requirement for all priests in the Western church.

Clericalism

It's hard to underestimate the power of the all-male culture of the Catholic clergy. This culture originates and is still dominated by an idealised but profoundly distorted theology of priesthood originating in a movement in seventeenth century France, begun by Cardinal Pierre de Bérulle (1575-1629) and Jean-Jacques Olier (1608-1657), pastor of Saint-Sulpice in Paris. Neither is well-known in the English-speaking world, but both have had profound influence on the spiritual identity and formation of the modern priest. It was Bérulle who developed the notion of the priest as *alter Christus*, a man so identified with Christ that he shared in Christ's very being, was literally ontologically changed into Christ. It's essentially the same kind of notion of priesthood proposed by John Paul II. As we've seen, Marie Keenan exposed for the RC the disastrous psychological consequences of this ideology.

Responding to the reforms called for by the Council of Trent, Olier – deeply influenced by Bérulle – established a seminary in the modern sense in his Parisian parish and then founded the Society of Saint-Sulpice (Sulpicians) to set-up and teach in seminaries. Olier's aim was to form educated, well-disciplined priests and the book attributed to him, *Traité des saints orders*, 'Treatise on Holy Orders' (it was actually edited by his second successor, Louis Tronson) became the key formation manual in seminaries worldwide before Vatican II. Olier professionalised the clergy long before lawyers and medical practitioners. The Sulpicians established the first two seminaries in North America in Montréal (1637) and Baltimore (1791). They've never been active in Australia, but the model came to Sydney via Ireland when Saint Patrick's College, Manly was established in 1889. The contemporary seminary system is based on and little changed from Olier's original. What is also significant is that this clerical ideology emerges at exactly the same time as Bellarmine's notion of the monarchical church.

Since Freud, it's certainly been true that there has been an emphasis on the centrality of sexuality in the human condition and this, together with modern psychology, has had an impact on the formation of clergy. A fundamental question has been: how does a priest integrate his sexuality into a celibate context? How does he convince himself that relationships with women and friends, marriage and family, are of secondary importance? How do celibates deal with sexuality, whether they be straight or gay? Deprived of normal emotional fulfilment, many priests live very isolated and lonely lives. Sure, it's possible for some men to be able to achieve a genuine, creative, celibate ministerial life, but not the large majority. Ministry involves priests in lives of generosity and self-giving and, while a false sense of messianism sustains some of them for some of the time, most priests have to face either emotional stultification and burn-out, or find a creative way of dealing with the ministerial and developmental demands that are placed on them.

There have been various proposed theological justifications for celibacy: Jesus remained unmarried, so priests as 'other Christs' should follow him. This ignores the fact that Jesus died when he was 33, long before he had to face the consequences of long-haul celibacy. It's also claimed that it frees men up for ministerial service, so that they are entirely focused on bringing God to others and serving them, undistracted by wife and family. This completely ignores the fact that the vast majority of Orthodox,

Anglican and Protestant clergy minister equally generously and effectively as married men or women, surrounded by wife or husband and children. Often, it's their marriages and families that sustains them in ministry and makes them more rounded persons.

A relatively recently justification for celibacy, borrowed from religious life, is that it is an 'eschatological sign' of heavenly life where 'men and women do not marry; no, they are like the angels in heaven' (Mark 12:25). However, using this text as a justification for celibacy is a distortion of the gospel. In this text, Jesus was actually talking about an internal Jewish dispute between the Pharisees who believed in the resurrection of the dead and the Sadducees who strongly denied it. It has nothing whatsoever to do with celibacy; it is Jesus arguing with various schools of rabbinical interpretation.

Whatever the justification for celibacy, the combination of seminary training, celibate formation and the deep-seated contradiction between a seventeenth century, clericalist notion of priesthood as articulated by Olier, and the real conditions of ministry in 21st century Australia sets up priests for an irreconcilable bind between the demands of modern ministry and a seriously outdated notion of priesthood. If you add to this the cultural contradictions and alienations that many recently-arrived foreign-born priests, formed in the old-style clericalist seminary, bring with them, you are setting-up a disastrous scenario for the Australian church.

A comment also needs to be made about an emerging coterie of conservative, hyper-orthodox, younger priests, so-called 'John Paul II priests'. Calling them 'young fogeys', sociologist-priest Andrew Greeley in a 2003 article says they seem 'intent on restoring the pre-Vatican II church and reversing the classic generational roles, [and] define themselves in direct opposition to the liberal priests who came of age in the 1960s and 1970s'. Greeley quotes fellow sociologist Dean R. Hoge's finding that 'half the newly ordained priests he encountered believe that a priest is fundamentally different from a layperson – that he is literally a man apart' and that the laity should learn respect for their priestly authority. 'Older priests', Greeley says, 'often complain that their younger colleagues are arrogant, pompous and rigid and that they love to parade around in clerical dress'.[30] Pope Francis has said that priestly formation must be 'a work of art, not a police action', and that the seminary should not be a place riddled with clericalism which he describes as 'one of the worst evils'. He says that the seminary 'must form... hearts. Otherwise, we are creating little monsters' who negatively impact the people of God. According to one US seminary rector, Francis is beginning to have an impact on the newest seminarians who are less clerical, more willing to engage with the culture around them and are committed to social justice and environmental issues.[31] We can only hope that this perception is correct.

Forgive me if I sound a bit 'I told you so', but I predicted in *Mixed Blessings* (1986) and more specifically in *No Set Agenda* (1991) that the Australian church had reached its *kairos*, a biblical word referring to the moment when hard decisions would have to be taken. Jesus begins his preaching in Mark saying 'The time has come' (1:15), by which he means the time for decision-making, the time to choose the kingdom of God. This is what *New York Times* religion writer, Peter Steinfels has called the contemporary 'Catholic moment'. In 1991, Australian Catholicism faced a similar 'moment', a creative crisis of opportunity to draw on our rich tradition to face up to the issues facing our society, like the search for identity and meaning and developing spiritual answers to 'the bankruptcy of individualistic, free market materialism'. But our church leadership led the church away from the challenge of dialogue and evangelisation into 'a safe and unquestioning sub-culture' largely focused on a small number of issues associated with gender, sexuality, abortion and, more recently, euthanasia.[32]

All that's happened since then is that things have got worse. In fact, Australian Catholicism is now facing an existential catastrophe, the worst in its history. The child abuse tragedy is the most obvious manifestation, but the church's malaise is deeper and more far-reaching. What the RC did was to confront Catholicism and not let church leadership off the hook. As Francis Sullivan says: 'Catholic Church leaders have railed against the fact that they are continually put in the frame as part of the problem. But the truth is that the church leadership for decades sought to deny this history [of sexual abuse]... They never fully acknowledged that the culture, structure, [and] processes of the Church were part of the problem... The trust and credibility in Church leaders has continued to decline, and... I think there's still the question, "Do they get it?"'[33] The answer to Sullivan's question is, as we'll see, is yes, they kind of get it, and no, they really don't!

Chapter Three
Models of Church

Mutating models of church

So far, there are two things the PC completely failed to tackle: first, a deep reflection on the nature of the church and ministry; and second, a thorough analysis of Australian culture and society. The failure to embrace these challenges means that the best that can be expected from the PC will be statements on particular issues, like support for the aspirations of First Nations people, or calls for women in decision-making and the establishment of parish and diocesan pastoral councils, or an emphasis on ecological conversion, or safeguarding and zero tolerance on child sexual abuse. All of these issues are important and while they give councillors and church leaders a sense that they have achieved something, in the end they will do nothing to stem the on-going decline of the church in Australia, because these are not the fundamental, underlying issues. A deeper theological and sociological analysis is essential.

First, ecclesiology, which involves a reflection on the nature of the church itself. This is the fundamental element that has been completely missing from the PC process. Archbishop Mark Coleridge was right when he told the ABC: 'I think the monarchical exercise [of episcopal control], that gathered to itself that culture of secrecy... that was so brutally exposed

[in] the Royal Commission, has got to go'.[34] That's the nub of the problem facing both the worldwide and Australian church: we are still operating out of a secretive, monarchical model that has long passed its use-by date. No matter what changes are made in governance, transparency or accountability, it will still be patching-up the old system, putting 'new wine into old wineskins', as Jesus said (Mark 2:22).

Let's be clear here: Jesus most certainly did not set-up a monarchical hierarchy. In the Gospels, he established a community of equal disciples, women and men, to carry on his mission of proclaiming the presence of the kingdom of God, by which he meant God's life-giving care for the whole of creation and God's loving involvement in history to bring humankind and all living things to salvation and fulfilment. As he told Pontius Pilate, 'My kingdom is not from this world' (John 18:36). Nevertheless, it must have seemed to his followers that everything came to a grinding halt when he died on the cross and his disciples must have shared his despair as he 'shrieked out', to translate Mark's text literally, 'My God, my God, why have you forsaken me' (Mark 15:34). But life conquered death and on the third day he was alive among them again, first proclaimed to the apostles by Mary Magdalene and the two women (Mark 16:1-7).

A kind of 'Jesus Movement' began at Pentecost, originally as a sect within Judaism, whose members were first called 'Christians' at Antioch (Acts 11:26). But a vision of God's kingdom and the message of Jesus needed structures of one sort or another to survive. So, right from the start, even in the later writings of New Testament itself, the lineaments of an institutional church began to emerge. But to survive, institutions also need to be dynamic, changing their shape to adjust to different historical conditions and this is certainly true for the church. Elsewhere, I've called these shifts 'mutations', which is a good word to describe what happened. The term comes from biology and refers to a genetic change where, in evolutionary terms, a new reality emerges, but this reality is still deeply rooted in and is the direct result of all that has gone before. In church history, there have been at least four major mutations in which the church has significantly changed shape.[35]

The first was when the early church emerged from its Jewish matrix to become a community for non-Jewish gentiles, a mutation that led to a conflict which is described in the New Testament in Acts of the Apostles, chapter 15. Originally, the dominant majority of Christians, led by James, were Jewish and they remained as a kind of sect within Judaism. But these Jewish Christians, like their compatriots, suffered in the two catastrophic Jewish revolts against Rome. The first in AD66-67 ended in the destruction of Jerusalem and the Temple, the centre of Jewish spiritual life. Then came the Roman defeat of Simon bar Kokhba's revolt in AD132, leading to widespread slaughter of Jews, including many Jewish Christians; their community was effectively destroyed. But Paul and other missionaries like Barnabas had already taken Christianity beyond the Jewish faith to the broader Greco-Roman world.[36]

Given the normative value of the New Testament and early church, we should closely examine this first mutation. Until the emergence of modern biblical and historical studies in the last two centuries, it was assumed that the ministerial model of a bishop, surrounded by presbyters (priests) and deacons could be discerned in the later writings of the New Testament. Nowadays, it is clear that the reality was much more complex. Up to about AD150, the structure of the church was quite fluid. Different forms of leadership developed in different places.

Rome and Antioch are examples. Antioch seems to have had a bishop earlier than other communities. In contrast, the Roman church was rather late in developing structures focused on a bishop; up to around AD140, there seems to have been a more collegial style of leadership in Rome. There was also significant tension in the early church between stable communities like the Judeo-Christians and travelling missionaries like Paul and Barnabas.

Once established, early Christian communities usually met in the houses of wealthy Christians, both women and men, although the recurrence of women's names in the New Testament is significant. Not only did the householders provide a place for worship; they often also provided the necessities for the gathering and may well have been the celebrants of the Eucharist. One of the earliest archaeological examples we have of a house church is in the excavations under the present church of San Clemente near the Colosseum in Rome. This is the house of Clement and it dates from the late-first century AD. Other references to house churches can be found in Paul's letters. The Letter to the Romans (AD57-58), for instance, is addressed to a house church owned by a couple named Prisca and Aquila who had worked with Paul in Corinth. Written there, he entrusted the letter to Phoebe, 'a deacon of the Church' (Romans 16:1), who was travelling to Rome and he sent special greetings to 'Prisca and Aquila... and the church in their house' (Romans 16:3-4). He issues a similar greeting in First Corinthians (1 Corinthians 16:19-20). The Letter to Colossae is addressed 'to the brothers and sisters in Laodicea, and to Nympha and the church in her house' (Colossians 4:15).

Some historians talk about "monarchical" bishops in the early church and refer specifically to Ignatius in Antioch (died c.AD107). He may well have seen himself as representing Christ as leader of the liturgy and teacher of the faith, but to use the term 'monarchical' in this context is a complete misnomer. He also seems to have been exceptional because, if anything, the New Testament suggests a kind of leadership by 'elders', a translation of the Greek πρεσβύτερος, or 'presbyter', which is nowadays sometimes used interchangeably with the word 'priest'. For instance, after a missionary journey through what is present-day Syria, Paul and Barnabas 'appointed elders for them [the converts] in each church... and entrusted them to the Lord' (Acts 14:23). There are numerous other New Testament references to elders and the word is always plural. To confuse things further, the Greek word ἐπίσκοπος ('episcopos'), the word we translate as 'bishop', was used interchangeably with elders. Certainly, by the late-second and early-third centuries, a common structure of bishop, advised by elders and assisted by deacons, had emerged across the local churches. But the main point I want to make is that there was nothing remotely monarchical in early Christianity; in fact, early church structures were, if anything, proto-democratic.

What is striking is the speed with which early Christianity took-off in the Roman world, especially in the eastern provinces. The attraction was that in Christ 'there was no longer Jew or Greek, no longer slave or free, there is no longer male or female; for all of you are one in Christ Jesus' (Galatians 3:28). This text was probably a baptismal formula rooted in the notion that the church is a place for everyone. Here was a welcoming community that gave even a slave equality with all other members of the community. This was especially important for women because the church discouraged early marriage and giving young girls to old men as brides. Christianity also opposed abortion, especially forced abortions and infanticide; killing female offspring was common practice in the late-Roman world.

In a highly stratified culture, the commandment of love was revolutionary and even subversive of the social order, as was the call to care for one another. The Christian community provided an escape from isolation and whatever their need, whether it be hunger, sickness, homelessness, poverty, or widowhood, Christians knew they would be supported by the community.

I have looked at the early church in some detail here because I believe that it has much to teach us as we face the future of Australian Catholicism. While no model of the church is absolute, the New Testament and the early church have normative value in church tradition and it's from this period that we should take our inspiration. Nevertheless, over the centuries, as it dealt with various social and political realities, the church adapted its structures to meet contemporary needs.

A key date in church history is 27 October AD312, the day Constantine defeated Maxentius, ruler of Italy, at Rome's Milvian Bridge on the Tiber. Constantine was sympathetic to Christianity and the Edict of Milan (February 313) granted toleration and legal recognition to Christianity. From being a proscribed and sometimes persecuted religion, Christianity mutated into the most important faith of the late Roman world. For the first time, the church was confronted with sorting out its relationship with the secular order. The result: the church was largely dominated by the state, especially in the Eastern empire, after Constantine moved his capital from Rome to Byzantium and renamed it Constantinople.

In the West, the Roman empire had pretty much collapsed by AD407 with the barbarian invasions, so the church was largely liberated from secular interference, but not before it had adopted many of the administrative lineaments of the late-Roman state. The breakdown of central administration in Western Europe in the fifth century meant that local churches retained autonomy in their internal affairs and bishops were elected locally, largely independent of Rome. Regional co-operation was maintained through synods that legislated for local regions. Rome was seen as the court of appeal in disputes and the touchstone and judge of orthodoxy.

The next mutation occurred with the high claims of popes like Gregory VII (1073-1085) to universal jurisdiction over the church and Europe. Gregory's successor, Innocent III (1198-1216) might claim that he was 'vicar of Christ... set midway between God and humankind', asserting that he'd 'been given the whole world to govern', but he lacked the wherewithal to project those claims outward because of slow or non-existent communications. He was probably dead before the news of his claims reached north-western Scotland, let alone Iceland. This was also this period that bequeathed us canon law which emerged from the revival of Roman law in the twelfth century. The key figure here is the monk Gratian (died c.1159) whose *Decretum Gratiani* or *Concordance of Discordant Canons* is the foundation of modern canon law. The result is that Catholicism became besotted with law, which has replaced the emphasis on love and service.

A late-medieval reaction to the focus on papal power was Conciliarism, a movement that strongly reflects the determination of medieval people to keep centralised power in check. The conciliar theory argued that the *congregatio fidelium* – the whole body of the faithful – was foundational to the church and it asserted the supremacy of the church community – especially when gathered in council – over the papacy and, by implication, over other hierarchs. It is a theory that nowadays merits a serious rethink.[37]

The monarchical mutation

While medieval elements like canon law have persisted until now, the model of church out of which we operate today essentially originates in the Reformation era and the political theory of absolute monarchy underpinned by an efficient bureaucracy, asserted by kings like Henry VIII, Francis I and Philip II. The notion of the 'divine right of kings' was the theory that kings were responsible to God alone and their will was the source of law. As we saw, these notions were applied to the papacy and church by Robert Bellarmine. He says unequivocally: 'The church of Christ is a most perfect kingdom and an absolute monarchy which neither depends on the people nor has from its origin, but depends on the divine will alone'.[38] The pope, Bellarmine said, cannot be judged, deposed, or punished by anyone, including a general council. The pope is supreme judge in deciding on faith and morals; what he teaches is, by that very fact, infallible.

It was this notion of papal monarchy that was embraced at the First Vatican Council in 1870 in which papal infallibility and, more importantly, papal primacy was defined. In the century between 1870 and Vatican II, papal authority was increasingly enhanced by forms of 'creeping infallibility' as everything the pope said took on ever-greater authority. Simultaneously, papal primacy increased as the Vatican gained centralised control over the worldwide church, especially through the Congregation of Propaganda Fide during the enormous missionary expansion of Catholicism in the nineteenth and first half of the twentieth centuries. Another key issue was that the Consistorial Congregation, now the Congregation for Bishops, gained almost complete control of the appointment of the world's bishops in the nineteenth century.[39] Prior to then, bishops were largely appointed locally. This change meant that usually only priests sympathetic to the official line prevailing in Rome would get the nod as bishops. This was a particularly disastrous policy with long-lived popes like John Paul II appointing men who lacked emotional intelligence and leadership skills, but who were orthodox 'yes' men who carefully followed the papal line. In the monarchical-hierarchical church, popes and bishops are not accountable to or transparent with the community, as this model prefers secrecy.

We are now at the tag end of the monarchical model which has far outlived its use-by date. No matter how often the PC talks about transparency, accountability and including laity – especially women – in ministry and decision-making, it will go nowhere because these notions are completely incompatible with absolutism.

'Light from the Southern Cross Report'

A chance to confront the monarchical model came with the 'Light from the Southern Cross Report' (LSCR). The RC had asked the ACBC to 'conduct a national review of the governance and management structures of dioceses and parishes, including in relation to issues of transparency, accountability, consultation and the participation of lay men and women. This review should draw from the approaches to governance of Catholic health, community services and education agencies'.[40] This led the bishops to set up a group to respond which eventually produced the 208 page LSCR that was delivered to the bishops in early May 2020, but kept confidential to allow them time to digest its contents. But it was quickly leaked and, after revisions, was finally published by the ACBC on 15 August 2020. The LSCR group was made up of seven members, with four international advisors. All are distinguished Catholics, mainly laypeople, and they had to work within a tight time frame with terms of reference focused on governance.

LSCR gets off to a good start with a quirky quotation from Henry Lawson and an introduction based on Saint John Henry Newman's comment – already cited – that 'In a higher world it is otherwise, but here below to live is to change, and to be perfect is to have changed often'. LSCR then quotes Pope Francis' response saying that change involves interior conversion, yet 'often we approach change as if it were a matter of simply putting on new clothes', window-dressing, without profound transformation.

While the report says it 'is not seeking to remake the Church in the image of corporate or civil entities', but only 'to identify existing good practice in the Catholic Church in Australia', modern governance buzz words recur like 'transparency', 'accountability', 'consultation' and 'participation'. Sure, it would be excellent if the hierarchy adopted these standards as embedded working norms, but the problem is that these words are derived from the processes of modern democracy, when the church is neither modern nor democratic. Its baroque, absolutist structure makes the pope a divine right ruler and each bishop a tinpot king in his own domain. The report assumes that modern governance principles can be grafted onto this absolutist system, but participative governance and absolutism are simply incompatible. The core problem here is ecclesiological; it involves different models of church. I don't blame the LSCR group for not addressing this; it was not in their remit. But the reality is that root and branch reform will not occur until this question is confronted.

The guts of LSCR are in the summary of recommendations (paragraph 2.7). These recommendations might have upset clericalist bishops, but left some more optimistic Catholics disappointed. For instance, regarding the appointment of bishops, the report recommends that 'the processes and procedures leading to the appointment of bishops by the pope be explained to the public'. Actually, the group Catholics for Ministry had done precisely that in 2011. It published the actual questionnaire the papal nuncio sent to carefully chosen 'consultants' to assess possible candidates for the Australian episcopate before he presented a *terna* (a shortlist list of three potential bishops' names) to the Congregation for Bishops.[41] LSCR also called for prior consultation, including analysing the needs of the diocese; that there be 'a wider consultation process leading to the creation of a *terna*, which should embrace genuine discernment that includes clergy and a larger number of lay people than is currently the case'. With the exception of a 'wider consultation process', this is little different from what already happens. In the end, everything still depends on decisions of the nuncio and Rome's Congregation for Bishops.

LSCR sets out detailed recommendations for the establishment of diocesan pastoral councils, finance councils and for holding diocesan synods. It emphasises the importance of lay review of diocesan expenditure and budgets. But there is no suggestion that members of these councils be freely elected by the faithful. They are appointed by the bishop. There are also calls for the inclusion of laity, particularly women, to appointments on diocesan decision-making bodies and agencies. One area where this is applied is in the selection and formation of candidates for the priesthood. Here, LSCR says, laity, including women, should play a decisive role in the selection, formation and training of candidates and deciding their suitability for ordination. This is a good move that might minimise the number of unsuitable candidates presently being ordained. Nevertheless, the faithful here are petitioning bishops, still working from the absolutist model.

One element of governance that the PC *must* put to the pope is the election of bishops by the local church. We have a long tradition in Australia of democratic elections, so there is no reason why we couldn't elect and call a bishop to a diocese, as does the Anglican church which, together with the Protestant Churches, could provide us with models and advice. The PC should also legislate that the local community call and appoint priests to parishes.

Despite the work of the LSCR, nothing substantial will change until Catholics face the reality that until the new wine of God's people on pilgrimage is poured into the new wineskins of a church built up from the community of baptised faithful. Otherwise we're just applying band-aids to the old absolutist structure. The time has come for the PC to tell Rome loudly and clearly: the monarchical model isn't fit for purpose; it has to go.

Beyond the monarchical model

What will replace the monarchical church? How do we get to a model which will integrate the values articulated by the LSCR while confronting the challenges of our culture creatively?

Here the vision articulated in the second chapter of *Lumen Gentium* (LG), Vatican II's Constitution on the Church, on the people of God and the community of the faithful on pilgrimage, is fundamental. God's people are drawn together by the Spirit, with each contributing their specific gifts to build up the church and the world. 'All... as a community and each according to their ability must nourish the world with spiritual fruits. They must diffuse in the world that spirit which animates the poor, the meek, the peace makers' (LG 38). Turning the old monarchical model on its head, Vatican II says that the local community is the basis upon which faith is built and expressed as we all participate in Christ's prophetic and priestly mission.

But Vatican II couldn't ignore the hierarchy, especially given that the Council was a meeting of some 2500 bishops! Chapter three of LG is devoted to 'those ministers who are endowed with sacred power' (LG 18), which largely espouses the absolutist model in contrast to chapter two. As I've argued in successive books since 1986, these chapters are mutually exclusive. Some try to hold them together in a kind of blancmange, but this creates the corrosive disjunction that we often experience in Catholicism; we talk the rhetoric of the people of God, but the institutional reality we face is absolutist. The problem is that a model of church based on a community of equals and one based on a clerical hierarchy are incompatible, even toxic and destructive. The resolution will only come when the emphasis is shifted from hierarchy to community.

Everything indicates that the monarchical model is in serious trouble with incompetent leadership, declining religious practice with only about 9% of self-declared Catholics attending Mass regularly and a collapse in local recruitment to the priesthood. Nevertheless, many contemporary Catholics – especially older people who experienced the pre-conciliar church – are already operating, mostly unconsciously, out of a Vatican II community model. All of our assumptions, the rhetoric we use, the kind of church we espouse, have already integrated the council. It's part of people's ecclesial DNA. That's why we experience such ecclesial disjunction because, in fact, we are so often dealing with the absolutist, Bellarmine model.

Until Catholicism tackles the issue of models, we'll simply be whistling in the wind. The PC may tinker at the edges, but what we now confront is the challenge of root and branch reform. We will only get this by shifting to a community model of church; the primary task of the PC should be to articulate for Australia a new way of operating based on the people of God model. It is within the context of this new model that we'll be able to actualise basic principles like accountability, transparency, full equality, involvement of the faithful, because this is where they fit like a glove. The real challenge is to articulate a future that is realisable and that provides hope.

The fact is that there are already a considerable number of church-related community models active in Australia. Jane Anderson has profiled these 'Innovative Catholics', as she calls them. Members' age range is from the late-fifties to the early-eighties, two thirds are lay people and a third laicised former priests and religious. There are three 'identifiable trajectories' among these groups: the 'meditation movement', the 'reform movement' and the 'advocacy movement'. What they have in common is that members feel 'that they are agents of their own destiny' and are 'active and collaborative'. There is much cross-over between them.[42]

The Christian Meditation Movement is widespread in Australia and there is a rising interest in meditation and contemplative prayer. While ecumenical, the large majority of leaders and members of the movement are Catholic. The second trajectory is that of Reformist Catholics. These are people inspired by Vatican II, and they tend to be more focused on the church itself, urging change in structures and governance, warning that Catholicism must 'adapt or die, move on or disappear'. The ACCCR typifies this trajectory. The third trajectory is the advocacy movement that is committed to playing an affirmative role in society where members work 'for victims of injustice, the poor and the marginalised and for raising ecological consciousness'.[43]

Most participants in these trajectories came to adulthood in the 1960s and 1970s, decades of activism and reform in society, particularly characterised by the Whitlam era (1972-1975). This was a time when people looked outward and believed in social justice and equity, were interested in going beyond themselves and building relationships. They were less preoccupied with the pathos of the individual and were more interested in structural inequity and the common good. This is not to idealise them, but simply to highlight their focus. Nowadays, just to form a community centred on social action in an individualistic era is counter-cultural.

The communities described by Jane Anderson provide both a model and foundation upon which a people-of-God-oriented church could be built. What should be the characteristics of new faith communities? They would be focused on the presence of Christ, rooted in the Catholic tradition and be outgoing, geared to ministry. The central focus must be Christ, the image and likeness of God. This is where the contemplative emphasis of the meditation movement is important. 'In their meditation', Anderson says, 'they navigate religious and social pressures through a spiritualised form of penetrating self-awareness that cultivates personal discipline and amicable connections' with others.[44] All genuinely Catholic communities must be committed to prayer and liturgy. They need to meditate on the scripture and 'break bread together' like the early communities in house churches. Everything they do must be inspired by the message and presence of Jesus.

Second, the new communities must be firmly rooted in the Catholic tradition. They are not beginning from scratch; they belong in an on-going communion of people incorporated into Christ through their baptism, a trans-historical communion of saints. They have a history and their challenge is to take that history and transform it to meet the needs of today. Third, a genuine Catholic community will always be geared to ministry. 'Ministry' here means outreach, a being with people, standing alongside them, as well as an engagement with the authentic issues of the day like global warming, ecological care and social justice. Whatever the ministry, it must reflect commitment to Christ in action, a building-up of the common good. The challenge for innovative Catholics is to begin the process of creating the new model of church based on the People of God in prayerful community, centred on Christ, rooted in tradition and dedicated to ministry.

Many existing communities like the ACCCR have dedicated their energy to the PC, saying they wanted to give the bishops one last chance. In my view, the bishops have had their chance and have failed. Leadership has now devolved to the laity and to the clergy and religious supporting them. The time has come to move on. Jesus sends out the 'seventy others... ahead of him to every town and place where he himself intended to go' (Luke 10:1). There is a real sense in which Jesus' committed followers must now go out like the seventy disciples leaving behind the monarchical-Bellarmine style church to prepare the 'towns and places', the contemporary secular world, for the coming of Jesus and his message. They go as 'lambs among wolves', building new communities – the better word here is communions – that begin to model a way of being church that is rooted in the New Testament and early Christianity and therefore firmly in the Catholic tradition, but which is geared to a secular, individualistic and very troubled contemporary world.

It is to that world that we will now turn.

Chapter Four
The Secular World

Religion in Australian culture

The PC has almost completely ignored Australian culture and society, the broader world within which Catholicism lives and proclaims the Christian message. There's been no forensic examination of what's is happening in the wider community and how, as believers, we might respond. The recent Australian Census certainly indicated that Christianity and Catholicism are in decline, given that the 'No Religion' category was up from 12.9% in 1991 to 30.1% in 2016, or just over seven million people. For those aged between 18 and 34, the 'No Religion' category scored 39.4%. The overall Christian proportion in 2016 was 52.1%, or 12.2 million people, a drop from 88.2% in 1966 and 74.0% in 1991. Some of this non-Christian increase is due to immigration.

Does this indicate, as some maintain, that Australia is becoming a secular wilderness, anti-church and anti-religion, with secularists trying to drive faith completely into the private sphere? This is not a new claim. In the late-19th century Australia was described as 'the most godless place under heaven', despite reasonably high practice rates among all the Christian churches. Nowadays, Australia is certainly becoming more secularised and anti-Catholicism particularly has deep roots in our history. Also, an anti-religious strain of secularism has emerged that seems to want to exclude religion totally from public life, to enforce a version of what the French call *laïcité*.

No one disputes that Australia is secular in the sense that the state has adopted religious neutrality, while allowing religious pluralism to flourish in the public square. Various forms of belief or unbelief are choices that citizens can make for themselves. Almost uniquely in the world, the Australian state financially supports religious-based education, health, aged care and social welfare. We live in a multifaith, multicultural society where belief and unbelief co-exist, guided by personal conscience. Canadian philosopher Charles Taylor describes this as a form of secularised society 'in which faith, even for the staunchest believer, is one human possibility among others'.[45]

However, there's still a pervasive feeling abroad that religion is eroding as people search for their own meaning structures and personal ethics. A note of caution is needed here. Catholic practice rates in Australia have always been historically lower than many think. If you take Mass attendance as a sign of more than nominal commitment, the Australian experience is that from 1820 when permanent priests arrived, an average of less than a quarter of all Catholics attended Mass regularly. For instance, in 1833 in the greater Sydney area, the figure was around 20%. From the 1850s to the 1940s, regular Mass attendance fluctuated between 20% to 30% of all Catholics. Except for the post-World War II period, when an extraordinary 75% of Catholics attended Mass weekly, affiliation has been decreasing since the late-1960s.[46]

The reality is that Catholicism has always had a high rate of nominal affiliation. In 2011, the practice rate was 12.2% (662,376 people), but by 2016 it had dropped to 11.8% (623,356 people), or 39,020 fewer attendees. Of regular attendees, 37% were born overseas and these new arrivals saved Mass attendance from serious decline. Even more worrying is the loss of young people: only 5.8% of 15- to 24-year-olds attend regularly, while 45.3% are over 60 years. Women account for 61.8% of all attendees.[47] If the church continues to alienate women, these numbers will decrease rapidly.

In the last two decades, a more aggressive secularism has begun to emerge. Religious terrorism, symbolised by the 9/11 attack, and the growing revelations of sexual abuse, particularly in the Catholic church, has led to public anger and antipathy towards religion. In the mainstream media, there is a certain element of secularist bias, particularly against Christianity and Catholicism. Part of it is due to a decline in religious literacy among journalists, where caricatures often replace knowledge. Christian feasts like Christmas and Easter have become secularised holidays with the transcendent meaning of their symbolism drained away.

You don't have to be conservative to say that Australia specifically and the Western world generally has lost its cultural bearings and entered a kind of identity crisis characterised by a loss of confidence in our religious, political, financial and social institutions. We no longer know what we stand for; we can't even agree on what it is we have in common. There is a kind of everyone for herself spirit abroad, as we struggle to find a set of values that provide us with a baseline to define ourselves. We kid ourselves that Australia is 'the land of the fair-go' where we hope that looking after mates in a tolerant multicultural mix will provide us with a societal baseline. We forget that living in a democracy requires a certain robustness, a willingness to tolerate even views that repulse us; democracy isn't a place for shrinking violets and it requires an intelligent and informed discernment.

Australia nowadays seems to be characterised by exactly the opposite. You see this illustrated in the media, and even more so in social media. Editorial discernment is lost in a 24-hour news cycle in which 'the trivial and significant, the relevant and the banal, truths, half-truths and lies [are] all cobbled together without the slightest discrimination between what matters and what doesn't'.[48] Truth in social media is determined by 'likes' and 'dislikes' and the internet is an amalgam of top-quality, well researched information and opinion, and ill-informed, ignorant and misleading detritus. In the process, everyone has become their own 'expert' on seemingly everything, especially after a quick glance at Wikipedia.

The argument is that secularisation has led to de-Christianisation. Personal freedom, individualism, the absolute validity of our wishes and desires, an end to discrimination, tolerance, gender equity and equality for all are now the guiding moral underpinnings of our society. It's claimed that none of these values need religion, faith or Christianity for support or validation; they stand on their own.

The Protestant theologian, Wolfhart Pannenberg, disagrees. He rejects the notion that a viable society can be built on an absence of religion and says that a purely secular culture lacks the sanctions that underpin and govern moral life. All that's left, he says, is 'the coercive power of the law'. He argues that 'a morality based on reason alone, independent of any religious connection, is... precarious... a sustainable social morality requires a religious basis'. Pannenberg says that when religious indifference becomes an integral part of public culture, it leads to a loss of consensus regarding moral and cultural values, which in turn leads to social disintegration and even tyranny. Pluralism, he says, makes sense in a situation in which competing claims to truth are treated with respect.

However, he rejects a pluralism which maintains that there is no such a thing as truth. While Pannenberg supports the separation of church and state, this should never mean the separation of religion from public life and he warns against completely 'adapting Christian faith and life to the demands of secularism'. But religious fundamentalism is not the answer either, but rather 'a strong re-affirmation of the central articles of Christian faith against the spirit of secularism and...a renewed commitment to rationality'. Integral to this faith and reason approach is Christian ecumenism, as the churches join together to proclaim the message of Jesus, while maintaining the unique gifts that each of them has to bring. Pannenberg says that the church communities are central to the response to the secularist dominance of culture. They are 'the reference point[s] of Christian existence'.[49]

Personally, I'm persuaded that Pannenberg's argument that morality does need a religious sanction to underpin it is correct, as is his argument that, without religion, all that is left is the coercive power of the law. His reference to fundamentalism is also relevant here. There is an increasing tendency in the media to identify religion with its most fundamentalist forms, the kind of approach much favoured by Richard Dawkins. The simple reality is that outside the ABC religion department, there are precious few religiously literate journalists.

Catholicism has only itself to blame for its failure in the media given its dereliction in dealing with sexual abuse and the failure of its leadership to present an even remotely inviting image to the public. The 'boots and all' approach of some bishops, the endless harping on a few issues around gender, abortion and euthanasia and the seeming inability of church leaders to engage in dialogue with others who don't share their views, leaves the religious space pretty empty.

Nowadays there's only a few public Catholics left to speak for the church community, like Frank Brennan, Francis Sullivan and, occasionally, yours truly.

The failure to respond adequately to the popularity of the 'new atheists' who flourished for about a decade in the early 2000s added to a sense of religious irrelevance. Richard Dawkins' *The God Delusion* (2006) and other best-selling books by Daniel Dennett, Christopher Hitchens and A. C. Grayling re-enforced this feeling. These writers seem obsessed with God; they're the ultimate 'God botherers'. Their speciality is demolishing the religious straw men they themselves construct, rather than tackling serious religious thinkers and theologians. They reduce all religion to fundamentalism and then proceed to ridicule what is already ridiculous. Richard Dawkins is a past master at this kind of *reductio ad absurdum*. In Australia, various pro-secularist groups are also pre-occupied with halting what they perceive to be the political influence of the churches.

Individualism

However, the real threat to faith comes not from atheism, but from the kind of individualism represented by a sense that my primary loyalty is to myself. In an age dominated by psychology, we have become self-engrossed to an extent that previous ages never were. Our obsessive concern with personal subjectivity makes it difficult to maintain an emphasis on the importance of community and the common good. In the individualist worldview, society exists primarily to meet my needs and demands and to protect my rights and privileges. Any sense of obligation to the community runs a poor second to *numero uno*. First emerging in the early 1970s, individualism has now morphed into the kind of obsessive self-centeredness that constantly appeals to personal needs, feelings, rights and hurts.

The subjectivist world of social media, manipulated by the mathematical algorithms that hook in the immature, inexperienced and gullible, has extended and deepened contemporary individualism. In this on-line world, people project their *personae*, their ideal images, almost to the exclusion of the exterior world. Through social media, we construct inflated digital images of our idealised selves that others can admire. Social media platforms like Twitter encourage us to think that our instant opinions and biases are monumentally important and others need to hear them. The more aggressive and extreme these opinions are, the better for the corporations that run social media, because this creates reaction and anger, keeping people online longer so more information about them can be harvested and sold on. In the process, this anger and aggression leads to an increasing collapse in the standards of public discourse.

The reality is that social media can lead to obsessive, narcissistic individualism. This was cleverly and prophetically highlighted in the far-sighted 1995 movie *To Die For*, starring Nicole Kidman, about a ruthless young woman who is prepared to do anything, including murdering her husband, to become a TV anchor-person. Her classic line in this well-scripted movie is: 'You're not anybody in America unless you're on TV... Because what's the point of doing anything worthwhile if nobody's watching? And if people are watching, it makes you a better person'. That's also the essence of so much social media.

But the loss of a sense of the common good and social responsibility is not just confined to individuals. It's also present in many of our major institutions and politics. The litany of scandals and law-breaking in the finance industry and banks shows a complete lack of social conscience. Again, it was a movie that captured this. Oliver Stone's 1987 film *Wall Street* has the classic speech by Gordon Gekko, played by Michael Douglas, on greed. In a sense the speech is a caricature, but it's worth quoting at length: 'Greed, for want of a better word, is good. Greed is right. Greed works. Greed clarifies, cuts through and captures the essence of the evolutionary spirit. Greed in all its forms, greed for life, for money, for love, knowledge, has marked the upward surge of mankind'. Gekko's protegee, Bud Fox, played by Charlie Sheen, eventually finds his conscience and asks Gekko: 'How much is enough?' Gekko replies: 'It's not a question of "enough" pal, it's a zero-sum game. Somebody wins, somebody loses'.

Too often, it's nature, biodiversity and the environment that loses. For years now, we've watched oil and coal companies fund global warming deniers. In Australia, Kenneth Hayne's Bank Royal Commission revealed that 'Greed was omnipresent as the scandals played out... Billing customers for no service. Charging the dead. Opening fraudulent Dollarmite [youth saver] accounts in children's names. Giving executives bonuses of 300%. Lending in a way that crippled the disadvantaged and unemployed. Greed, every time'.[50] As Hayne himself put it: 'Too often, the answer seems to be greed – the pursuit of short-term profit at the expense of basic standards of honesty'. While we can't eliminate greed and dishonesty, governments can at least regulate and police it. When they fail to do that, people become alienated from society and even from democracy itself.

Post-modernism

While individualism is inherent in human nature, in contemporary Western culture it has been enhanced by the ideology of post-modernism. This jargon word is hard to define because it's really a hotch-potch of ideas centring around the notion that today people reject so-called 'metanarratives', the big, overarching meaning structures, stories and ideas that we use to interpret our lives, the beliefs that help us make sense of our existence. Christianity is a metanarrative, Marxism another, democracy another. Ironically, post-modernism itself is a metanarrative because it asserts the universal notion that there are no metanarratives! It also asserts that there is no capital-T Truth, there are no right or wrong interpretations, just the facts of your life; in the end, reality is what you make of it. 'You have your way. I have my way. As for the right way, the correct way and the only way, it does not exist', to quote Friedrich Nietzsche. Philosopher Jean-François Lyotard says that post-modernism is not a philosophy, but an analysis, a diagnosis of what is actually happening in contemporary society.[51] There's some truth to that. Post-modernism claims that all the old ways of understanding reality have passed their use-by date and the only reference points we have left are those we construct for ourselves. 'There are no facts, only interpretations', to quote Nietzsche again. All we can do is embrace the temporary, subjective, personal experiences that make-up the structure of our individual and group lives.

In a way, Donald Trump is post-modernist in that he creates his own moral framework, ignores objective science and ethical norms with the blunt assertion that his individual decisions need no external validation. He instinctively understands his political base and how to use publicity and social media to pander to their needs and prejudices. His lies, 'alternative facts', vulgarity, superficiality and anti-intellectualism have made him an archetype of post-modernism inhabiting a post-truth world in which there is no objective reality. Trump was maintained in the presidency by a bevy of officials, many of whose actions and attitudes reflected his own lack of moral conscience. A few, like FBI Director, James Comey, whom Trump sacked in 2017, had the integrity to stand up to him, but most knuckled under, using Trump for their own advancement.

Trump may be gone, but the threat to democracy has not. We find the same type of dishonesty, lying, corrupt behaviour, pork-barrelling amounting to billions of dollars, disinformation, lack of transparency and accountability and a failure to act with integrity in Australia. In a report 'The risks to Australia's democracy' the Washington, DC-based think-tank, The Brookings Institution, warned in January 2021 'that long-standing complacency with respect to governance standards, deep public ignorance about the proper workings of institutions, and arguable overreach by various levels of government without accountability for such overreach is worryingly evident' in Australia. Brookings also found that 'the standing of democracy amongst Australians... is not overwhelmingly positive'. In a recent poll of Australian attitudes towards democracy, it is troubling that 30% of 18–29-year-old citizens surveyed 'believed a non-democratic system is preferable to a democratic one under some circumstances'. Fortunately, this is not reflected among more mature people, but the trend is worrying nevertheless.[52] A radical spiritual commitment to community, truth, justice and equity seems incongruous in this kind of cultural atmosphere.

Religion in Australia

We also live in a culture that, in an attempt to embrace a secular form of multiculturalism, has largely repudiated its Christian roots. Progressives dismiss Christianity as passé and replace it with substitute movements of various sorts focused around rights of minorities, reconciliation, or various other causes. As Guy Rundle says: 'Perhaps you need to have had a religious education to understand... that even our secular life is shot through with Christian understandings of the world, of the power of myth, that modern politics is founded in parable'.[53] The clue here is Rundle's reference to 'religious education'. What has happened is that modern education has marginalised the religious element in our culture and history.

This is borne out in an interesting 2018 study by scholars at the ANU, Deakin and Monash Universities, the AGZ Study, that looked specifically at the religious attitudes of Gen Z teenagers between the ages of 15 to 16 and more generally those aged 13 to 18.[54] The study found 'a complicated picture of faith and spirituality among young Australians' which researchers divided into six 'spirituality types'. The first are the 'this-worldly' who have no space in their worldviews 'for religious, spiritual or non-material possibilities... [They] don't identify with a religion'. For them, science is important. They account for 23% of Australian teens. The second group account for 17% and they are the 'religiously committed'. For them 'religious faith, whether... Christian (mainly Pentecostal and evangelical), Islam or something else, is a big part of their lives'. They attend worship services regularly and their faith 'is important in how they shape their lives'. Here it's worth noting that there are insufficient numbers of Catholic teens for the researchers to mention them among the 'religiously committed'. But back to the study: The third group are 'the seekers' comprising 8% of teens. They have 'a decidedly eclectic worldview, seeking out their spiritual truth... they identify with a religion and believe in God or a higher being'.

The researchers point out that these three groups 'represent decisive groups'. The next three groups comprise those who lean toward one or other of the first three groups, 'but with less conviction'. The fourth group are the 'spiritual but not religious' comprising 18% of Australian teens. 'God, faith and religion are not important to them, but the door is open to spiritual possibilities... and belief in a higher being (but not really God)'. Then there are the 15% 'indifferent', those who don't care, or who are undecided about it all. The final group are the 'nominally religious' who follow their parents or their school community's religion, whether Catholic or Islamic. They 'identify with a religion and believe in God, but faith is not important in their daily lives and they don't often darken the door of a temple, church or mosque'.

A more optimistic scenario for Christianity is painted in McCrindle Research's *The Future of the Church in Australia* (2020) and *Australia's Changing Spiritual Climate* (2021).[55] Both reports say that disillusionment with the churches is widespread in Australia, but that people want something more in their lives, like spirituality, community and connection. According to McCrindle, Australians are not anti-religious; they believe in God and search for ways to encounter the transcendent in their lives. While the church remains a problem, 'Australians are looking for more meaning than ever', Mark McCrindle says. 'They're searching for purpose, they're looking for certainty or direction in these uncertain times, they're spiritually open and they're looking for community more than ever before.'[56] The reports highlight the strong sense of religious affiliation in multicultural communities and it says that the churches need to re-establish trust and engage with the community on social issues.

However, I have problems with this. *The Future* report was constructed from thirty in-depth interviews with church leaders and an on-line survey of 1002 church-goers, most of them from across the Evangelical or Pentecostal spectrum. Only two Catholics were interviewed: Melbourne Archbishop Peter Comensoli and Daniel Ang, Sydney archdiocese evangelisation director. The report reflects its Evangelical-Pentecostal origins, presents an overly-optimistic picture that is not reflected in other reports like the AGZ study, and doesn't gel with experience. For sure, there is a secularist presumption in Australian media reporting on religion that Christianity is in serious decline and that people are abandoning belief. There is also evidence for a kind of spiritual hunger out there, but that doesn't let the churches off the hook. The McCrindle report really reflects the position of the 17% religiously committed teens in the AGZ study. Nevertheless, the prognosis for Christianity and Catholicism in Australia doesn't look good.

However, there are some positive notes. The religiously committed teens and the seekers together comprise 25% and when people tick a "no religion" box on the census, it doesn't mean they have abandoned all belief; it can mean they just don't want to be identified with a particular faith. Among adults, as well as teens, there are many people trying to craft or construct their own belief structure. Young people particularly want to find spiritual and communal lives that make sense to them. They are, in a literal sense, spiritual consumers who prioritise what is personally meaningful to them. They want to decide their own spiritual development.

But there's a flip side to this. Working out everything for yourself is an exhausting process and it's so easy to delude yourself. Individual meaning structures also make it difficult to form community. As people lose trust in democracy, governments and institutions like political parties, media, churches, unions, banks, big business and, most recently, the armed forces, they experience a loss of confidence. In a 2021 Essential Vision survey people had most trust in scientific bodies (68%) and health authorities (64%), an understandable response during a pandemic.[57] In 2020, it was the federal and state police at 68% who were most trusted, with the high court at 61%, the ABC at 58% and religious organisations at 35%, up from 28% in 2019.[58]

In a fast-paced society like ours, many cannot keep up. Inequality, social isolation, lack of social support, failure to exercise, overeating and widespread clinical depression lead many to feel disoriented and powerless to change the world's trajectory. We experience a sense that, as Hamlet says, 'The time is out of joint' (Act I scene 5). While this feeling has been around for several decades, it has been deepened by the threat of climate change, mass extinction and environmental degradation. Young people, see their future very threatened. 'We won't die of old age, we'll die from climate change', they say. Activist Greta Thunberg says: 'I don't want you to be hopeful. I want you to panic. I want you to feel the fear I feel every day. And then I want you to act'. Then along comes the pandemic with its fear of infection, lockdowns and restrictions on movement and activity, schools closed, financial stress, remote work, or worse, no work at all, together with an apprehension of threat that seems to be completely out of our control. Many have experienced depression and loneliness. Vaccination is our only protection, but with new strains emerging, the threat remains. It's all pretty depressing!

Searching for 'something more'

In 1969, the Australian poet and convert to Catholicism, James McAuley (1917-1976), wrote a poem 'In the Twentieth Century', that gives expression to the discordance and emptiness that many people experience. I used to meet him occasionally in the early 1970s in Hobart where he was Professor of English at the University of Tasmania. A conservative man, he had a profound conviction that modern scepticism had silenced the poetry of faith. He was convinced that Western, post-Christian society had lost a sense of tradition and with it, a feeling for spirituality and belief.

> Christ, you walked on a sea
> But you cannot walk in a poem,
> Not in our century.
>
> There's something deeply wrong
> Either with us or with you.[59]

The poem reflects McAuley's identification of faith with his understanding of 'tradition'.

I accept that it's difficult to talk openly about Christ today, because in the public secular sphere there's an unspoken rule that religious discourse must be kept purely private. It's even more difficult to speak openly about Christian belief and spiritual experience. Nowadays there's an unconscious but real conviction among many people that any form of faith is a retreat to fundamentalism and the poetry of belief is dismissed as superstition. There's no appreciation of the link between faith and reason and the investigation of belief by reason enlightened by faith. Instead, religion is treated as a personal consumerist choice, a purely private and somewhat idiosyncratic matter.

But all is not lost because many also experience dissatisfaction with the meaninglessness of so much post-modern existence. Greed doesn't work, doesn't clarify, doesn't cut through, isn't the meaning of evolution, doesn't mark 'the upward surge of mankind', Gordon Gekko notwithstanding. Neither does consumerism. McAuley says:

> Yet we dream of song,
> Like parables of joy.
> There's something deeply wrong.

'We dream of song', we long for what is better. Nevertheless, we still feel 'There's something deeply wrong'. In a sense, those lines capture the contradictions at the heart of our culture: we want what is good, generous and out-going, a world and community that cares for others and that is not heading to environmental oblivion. But we still feel that something is 'deeply wrong' as the utterly superficial nature of our culture evokes a restlessness that we long to escape.

This is where the church should enter bringing the poetry of faith into the picture. 'Religion is poetry or it is nothing!' cosmologist Thomas Berry says. 'How can a person be religious without being poetic... All the great mystics have been poets. You cannot do it any other way'.[60] What Berry is referring to here is the profound link between faith and imagination. Imagination is the ability to intuit the deeper realities and meanings underlying our experiences, the facility to conceive of other possibilities, the sense that the world we inhabit points beyond itself to deeper meanings, resonances and presences.

This is reflected in Jesuit Gerard Manley Hopkins' poem 'God's Grandeur':

> The world is charged with the grandeur of God.
>   It will flame out, like shining from shook foil;
>   It gathers to a greatness, like the ooze of oil
> Crushed.

God, Hopkins tells us, is to be found in the beauty and goodness of the world, but his imagery is strikingly unusual. The sense is that God's presence runs like a current through all of reality and it can be momentarily perceived in the lightening-like flashes of shook gold foil in the sun, or in the olives that only reveal their true selves when crushed. He gives us a clue when he says later in the sonnet 'nature is never spent' and as we look deeper, we discover that 'There lives the dearest freshness deep down things'. That is, beyond the surface superficialities, there is a deeper, poetic meaning that faith reveals, because faith, like beauty and great art, point beyond themselves to deeper meanings, presences and resonances. Imaginative perception in this sense is something intuitive whereby we grasp presences and meanings in nature and other people beyond conscious reasoning. Intuition is often based on deeply stored experience and knowledge. This has led to what US theologian David Tracy calls the 'analogical imagination', or the 'Catholic imagination', by which Tracy means a specific vision of reality that is shared by most Catholics.[61] It is, as Anglican theologian Graeme Garrett says, 'a cradling, and embracing way of thinking, willing and being, that you learn not so much with your head, but through other people who already have it and who mediate it to you via nurturing and formation'.[62] While many have moved beyond the church's doctrinal teaching, they still feel 'Catholic'; its more to do with imagination and feeling than reason. To some extent Catholic education is passing this formation on, but it is more likely to express itself these days through a spiritual commitment to nature, environmentalism and social justice than in something explicitly religious, like attending Mass regularly.

So, in summary, the culture in which we are proclaiming the Christian gospel is both self-engrossed, but restless for something 'more', a meaning structure, a spirituality. The challenge that confronts the PC and the church is how to relate the person of Christ, 'the image of the invisible God, the first-born of all creation' (Colossians 1:15) to the social and cultural reality of contemporary Australia. The next chapter will look at how that might be done.

Chapter Five

Proclaiming the Gospel in Australia

A more missionary church

One of the primary tasks the PC set itself was 'to develop concrete proposals to create a more missionary, Christ-centred Church in Australia at this time'. In a sense the Australian church has been attempting to do this for most of its history through the community's ministerial service to our fellow citizens in a whole range of areas. Throughout the nineteenth century and up until the late-1960s, most of this was provided by the religious orders, supported by laity, with minimal or no government support. The church's work in education, health, aged care, child care and social services – the Saint Vincent de Paul Society is an outstanding example of the laity in social service ministry – has been extraordinary. The situation changed in the early-1970s with the advent of state support for ministry in these areas, and the Catholic Church remains one of the mainstays of service provision to Australians.

However, reflecting on almost two hundred years of ministry to the community, it has to be said that much of this was carried out in institutions run on an almost industrial scale and that, especially for children, vulnerable people and their families, this led to situations in which sexual abuse occurred that left people damaged for the rest of their lives.

But the question remains as to whether care for the vulnerable and service to people in need is still approached in an industrialised and increasingly nowadays, bureaucratic way.[63] Whole government departments are now devoted to 'human services' and despite their best efforts, people are still treated as numbers. Because they need government funding, the churches and charities have gone along with political priorities and to a considerable extent have followed the money trail.

As a result, Australian Catholicism faces some tough questions regarding its vast ministerial structure. Is its sheer size sustainable? What does the church offer that is different to other comparable services? How do you integrate staff working in Catholic institutions who don't share Catholic ideals and ethos? What are the long-term consequences of government funding of work that the church sees explicitly as ministry? How does this relate to Jesus' model of personal service as he washed his disciples' feet (John 13:1-7)? Add to that the fact that 'Australian Catholicism is a "hollowed-out" institution with declining membership, mediocre leadership and a seventeenth century governance structure that is hopelessly inadequate in a pluralist society'.[64]

To prevent the church's ministries being perceived and actually becoming just outfits delivering government services, serious efforts have already been made to maintain the explicitly Jesus-based, ministerial focus of the church's work. Some really effective programs have been set-up. For instance, in the context of Catholic hospitals and health care, Susan Sullivan has developed programs for the ongoing formation of leadership and staff in the Christian vision of mission and ministry, emphasising care for the poor and vulnerable, an appreciation of people's work so that their gifts and talents flourish, and 'a way of understanding and being present to suffering... that supports courage, meaning and a belief in the afterlife'. She links this to a sense of the interdependence of all life, and 'a commitment to fostering and strengthening hope'. Sullivan says that this requires ministerial leaders 'actively placing Catholic identity and ethos at the heart of governance and leadership practices, the manner in which services are delivered [including]... culture and relationships'.[65] Other church bodies have developed strategies along similar lines to maintain the church's unique contribution to these ministries.

The PC says it wants 'to create a more missionary' church. 'Create' is the right word here, because for much of the history of Australian Catholicism we have merely 'passed-on' the faith from one generation to the next, primarily through schools and parishes. There was nothing creative about the process and any growth in the size of the Catholic population came largely from immigration and to a lesser extent, from fertility. Both the hierarchy and the Catholic community have largely seen it as their task to preserve the faith, rather than to evangelise the culture. What the PC is doing, albeit unconsciously, is challenging the church to go out into the world, as Jesus sent out the apostles and disciples (Matthew 10:5-25 and Luke 10:1-16) to proclaim the kingdom of God. He assured them that this would not be an easy task: 'I am sending you out like lambs into the midst of wolves'. Perhaps the wolves won't be quite so dangerous in Australia, but evangelisation still requires an intelligent, sophisticated approach in a rather unwelcoming secular society, especially given the church's current toxic reputation. What I want to do here is to develop some strategies to approach evangelisation in Australia, because this is a task the PC failed to address.

The early church and evangelisation

Here the early church has something to offer us. It was enormously successful, growing from a small, frightened group of disciples of a crucified Jesus, to becoming a numerically important religion in the late-Roman world when Constantine seized power in AD312. As historian Marta Sordi says during those 280 years the church suffered intermittent persecution by the state, but that 'general persecution organised by the ruling powers throughout the empire' was rare, but that 'there were small, localised persecutions fomented and often carried out by the mob', as well as there being 'long periods of tolerance'.[66] By AD300, Sordi says, there were more than six million Christians, centred mainly in the eastern provinces, in an empire-wide population of 44 million, although other historians cite much lower figures of about five million around AD400.[67]

How did this growth happen? There is no simple answer to this question. Clearly, the stable and organised infrastructure of the empire helped with good roads, a reliable shipping system and Greek and Latin being the common languages spoken across society. Christians could move around, and did. Early on, the Jewish synagogue system in the diaspora provided a basis for apostles like Paul and Barnabas. There was also the clear commission from the risen Christ to 'Go and make disciples of all nations baptising them... and teaching them everything I have commanded you', with the reassurance that 'I am with always to the end of the age' (Matthew 28:19-20). There is also a sense in which the empire was a religiously tolerant society, with many beliefs, sects and philosophies flourishing, although the imperial government drew the line with those who didn't observe *religio*, the accredited and authorised state cult. Carrying out the state rituals which connected Roman society to the gods was the important element. The cult was based on honouring the ancestors, the emperor and Dea Roma, the female deity of Rome. *Superstitiones*, superstitious private beliefs like Judaism and Christianity, were tolerated as long as they didn't interfere with participation in *religio*, the official cult. It is precisely in this intersection that Christians sometimes got caught and it was their failure to carry out *religio* that led to the legal proscription of their faith and to persecutions.

However, we should not idealise the early church as through it experienced no conflicts or divisive disputes. An example was the late-second century Montanist movement, a group that has much in common with present-day Pentecostals and charismatics. The Montanists believed that their prophets and prophetesses gave voice to an outpouring of the Holy Spirit in the church and they claimed that church authorities were repressing this outpouring. They looked forward to a Heavenly Jerusalem appearing in Phrygia, present-day central-western Turkey. In many ways the Montanists were an early apocalyptic movement reacting against the institutionalisation of Christianity. Despite Paul's warning 'Do not quench the Spirit, do not despise prophesying' (1 Thessalonians 5:19), even the early church authorities were suspicious of too much religious enthusiasm, let alone inspired or prophetic frenzy.

Several scholars have examined the rapid spread of Christianity.[68] The first was Adolph von Harnack, whose *Mission and Expansion of Christianity*, published in German in 1902, attributed the success of Christianity to the fact that it included in its ranks people from every stratum of society, from the imperial court to slaves. It also drew these people into a genuine community of equals from the highly stratified and inherently violent late-Roman society. It also offered a demanding ethic and an answer to meaning of life questions and celebrated liturgies that drew the community together around baptism and the living presence of Christ in the eucharist.

Michael Green acknowledges Harnack's insights, but concluded that it was primarily the personality of Jesus who drew converts into the church. Jesus' worldview was a revolutionary message of love, forgiveness and service of others and Green argues that Christians reflected that worldview in their own lives. They were seen by their contemporaries as very dedicated and, at times, were willing to die for their commitment. This is reflected in Tertullian's (c.160-c.225) comment that their contemporaries were impressed because 'Christians love one another and are willing to die for each other'.[69] A more recent scholar, Rodney Stark, takes a more sociological and demographic approach, arguing that Christian communities had higher birth rates because they outlawed abortion and infanticide, and they attracted many women because they offered equality when women's role was largely limited to home and family in households dominated by men. In the Christian community, slaves were treated as equals when, in the rest of society, they were denied all civil and legal rights. Given the large number of slaves in Roman society, this made Christianity attractive to them.

Beyond these more personal issues, the church developed a sophisticated formation in faith, the catechumenate. Conversion to Christianity and preparation for baptism was a thorough process that was neither quick nor easy. Catechumens remained with the community during the liturgy of the Word, but left before the Eucharist was celebrated. In the Lenten lead-up to baptism at Easter, they underwent a series of scrutinies, or formal tests, as well as fasting and prayer. Baptism was always celebrated within the liturgical context of the Easter Vigil and it was by total immersion. The whole process was seen as an entry into the death and resurrection of Christ. They were then anointed, the community laid hands on them, the kiss of peace was exchanged and finally they were admitted to the Eucharist. The long formation process made sure that converts were properly initiated into the faith.

The early church also developed a coherent public apologetic defending Christian faith, as believers attempted to explain themselves in terms of Greco-Roman culture.[70] Genuine Christian belief is always grounded in reason, by which I mean a faith that is integrated into full human development, making the believer a better person. Sure, it has an intellectual, rational component which seeks to understand itself within the context of the realities and cultural priorities of the contemporary world. It is a faith that is able to talk sensibly to contemporaries about what is truly important in life.

Application to contemporary Catholicism?

I said earlier that the Australian church, while providing extraordinary service to the general community, was largely preoccupied with handing on the faith through school and parish to the emerging generation, rather than evangelising the culture. Also, until about 1960, religious affiliation had a semi-racial basis. The Irish were Catholics, the Scots Presbyterian, the Welsh Methodist, the Germans Lutheran, the English Anglican. In this broadly Christian, but sectarian, context in which Catholicism operated before Vatican II and modern ecumenism, this maintenance approach was understandable and was really the basis of a kind of 'Catholic ghetto'. Nowadays, the world has changed radically and the growing 'no religion' category in the census tells us we are facing a very different cultural context in the 2020s from Australia up to the 1960s.

In a way, the early church had it easy. It was a new faith entering a world of already established religions. While they would have known something about Judaism, the Romans didn't have established presuppositions about Christianity. But nowadays, in a non-religious, secular culture that to a considerable extent repudiates its Christian roots and often caricatures them, we're not working with a blank canvas and older maintenance approaches no longer work. In fact, the evidence from the AGZ Study shows that 52% of Gen Z teens (the generation from the mid to late-1990s to around 2010) simply don't identify with religion at all. While 19% identify with Catholicism, 'in terms of attendance at services of worship, 58% of teens never attend, and just 12% attend weekly or more often. Pentecostals, Muslims, conservative Protestants and other kinds of evangelical Christians are the groups mostly likely to attend with any kind of regularity', but not Catholics.[71] As Joe Mulvaney told *We Are Church Ireland*, 'Catholic parents know that it is not possible to evangelise [young people] today in the language of sexism, misogyny, homophobia, or patriarchal monarchy'.[72] The church is losing Gen Z, just as it lost many of the Millennials.

There is a real sense that nowadays Christianity and particularly Catholicism is beginning from well behind scratch. Many of our contemporaries have established views on Christianity and especially the Catholic Church. Christianity is seen as passé, a religion whose time has run out; this is re-enforced by identifying Christian belief with its most fundamentalist forms, which are viewed as espoused by self-interested pressure groups that want to marginalise those who don't identify with their repressive approaches to gender, sexuality and life issues. The church is seen as even more toxic, due primarily to the sexual abuse crisis, and secondarily to Catholicism's seeming repudiation of the issues that are most important to our contemporaries, issues like the acceptance of the changing role and radical equality of women throughout society, acceptance of gay marriage and LGBTQIA+ people, and the right to euthanasia. These are non-negotiable issues for many people today and their rejection by church leaders and some church people renders their faith and beliefs irrelevant. People have just stopped listening to the church.

Pre-evangelisation – the search for common ground

So how then do we find common ground to communicate and dialogue with contemporary Australian culture? First, rather than trying to convert people, we need to build bridges and learn to talk to our fellow citizens. We need to look for common causes and how we can work together to improve our society and environment. Otherwise, even a justified critique based on the gospel and the church's social tradition will be seen simply as a rejection of contemporary values. It is only after having established relationships that we might be in a position to get people to listen to us, let alone see us as worth joining. It is the dialogue that is important, not massive numbers of conversions.

What we can learn from the early church is an emphasis on the centrality of Christ and his message of love, reconciliation and forgiveness, as well as establishing a community that cuts across social barriers and that accepts all community members as equal. This is certainly the direction in which Pope Francis is moving the church. He is turning Catholicism away from an idealised and unreal model of marriage and fidelity toward finding ways of welcoming Catholics whose lives are seen by some as not quite measuring-up to the ideal and are deemed 'irregular'. We're talking here about divorced-re-married Catholics, gay and lesbian couples and unmarried people living together 'in sin', all returning to Communion. Many of these Catholic people have felt ostracised by the church. They need to be welcomed back. Closely linked to this is the need for the church to recognise the absolute equality and centrality of women in the Catholic community and their access to all of the church's ministries. Formation in faith, prayer and liturgy is also fundamental to a lively church community that is supportive of its membership while, at the same time, being open to the world and serving it through ministry.

As I said, to be able to proclaim Christ effectively in a pluralist society like Australia, the church has to find common ground to be able to talk to our fellow citizens. This is more than just talking points on which we might agree to differ; it involves causes and issues through which we all commit to work together to improve the world and society. By far the most important of these challenges for all of us, both the churched and the secular, is the constellation of questions making up the ecological crisis, including global warming, biodiversity loss and human overpopulation.

Even Popes John Paul II and Benedict XVI had concerns about environmental degradation, but it was Pope Francis, especially in the Encyclical *Laudato Si'* (2015) who really highlighted the issue. He told the Council of Europe in September 2021 that the importance of caring for our common home was 'a universal principle that involves not only Christians, but every person of good will who has the protection of the environment at heart'.[73] He says perceptively that 'The problem is that we still lack the culture needed to confront this crisis. We lack leadership capable of striking out on new paths and meeting the needs of the present with concern for all and without prejudice towards coming generations'. He emphasises the importance of protecting the natural world within the context of an international 'legal framework which can set clear boundaries and ensure the protection of ecosystems'. Otherwise, he warns 'new power structures based on the techno-economic paradigm may overwhelm not only our politics, but also freedom and justice' (*Laudato Si'*, 53).

The church has to be part of what Greta Thunberg calls 'cathedral thinking'. She told the European Parliament that we need 'a far-reaching vision' which 'will take courage. It will take a fierce determination to act now to lay the foundations where we may not know all the details about how to shape the ceiling. In other words, it will take "cathedral thinking"'.[74] It is precisely in developing this kind of approach that the church has a foundation for a genuine dialogue with our fellow citizens who are deeply concerned about ecology and all the consequences of our misuse and abuse of the natural world. This is the issue which the church can link Christian belief and commitment to the major concern of our culture. It is to the credit of the Plenary Council that it at least attempted to address global warming and to focus on the need for 'ecological conversion', a term used frequently in *Laudato Si'*. The term actually originated in Australia in the work of Dennis Edwards and in my own *God's Earth* (1995).[75]

Unfortunately, the PC didn't make the connection between the church and secular society in addressing these issues, when it is precisely here that we have extraordinary agreement between the church and secular society.[76] It is true that the bishops have established an agency within their Commission for Social Justice, Mission and Service called Catholic Earthcare. Its web page highlights ecological spirituality, ecological economics, developing a sustainable lifestyle and carbon neutrality, and it has practical material for developing parish and schools-based programs for discussion and formation. But, perhaps understandably, it doesn't confront the key challenges that are politically and economically important. Here I'm referring to problems like dealing with the future of coal, oil and gas, logging of old growth forests, biodiversity loss like the endangered status of koalas due to the voracious demands of land developers, spreading of human settlement into the forests on which these animals depend. Increasingly, Catholics will have to bring our moral tradition to focus on these issues.

Pope Francis has given the lead here. *Laudato Si'* makes it clear that, while pollutants like coal, oil and gas might be briefly used to tide us over in the short term, they must 'be progressively replaced without delay' (para. 165). He also criticises the plundering of earth's resources 'because of short-sighted approaches to the economy, commerce and production'. He focuses particularly on 'the loss of forests and woodlands' which are being used 'merely as potential "resources" to be exploited, while overlooking the fact that they have value in themselves. Each year sees the disappearance of thousands of plant and animal species which we will never know, which our children will never see, because they have been lost for ever' (paras 32-33). Francis is placing these issues squarely within the context of morality and ethics and it is precisely in this context that Catholics must become active. It needs to be said clearly that environmental exploitation and destruction involves serious *sin*. I use the word 'sin' here deliberately because destroying the natural world is evil and we need to get beyond the kind of squeamishness that characterises so much contemporary ethical rhetoric these days as people hesitate to confront thuggery and destructive behaviour.

As I argued in 1995 in *God's Earth*, logging old growth forests is sinful, especially since we've already lost more than 75% of them. If you ever wanted up-to-date proof of this kind of destructiveness, you only have to look at what the Jair Bolsonaro government in Brazil is allowing to happen in the Amazon rainforest. The Brazilian bishops said recently that the rainforest 'has been handed over by the federal government to deforesters, arsonists and miners, gold seekers... who kill and terrorise indigenous peoples, destroy forests, pollute rivers and seriously poison organisms with mercury'.[77] Although he says he is a Catholic, Bolsonaro's rhetoric resonates with that of Donald Trump and with Brazil's growing number of evangelical Protestants.

But you don't have to go to Brazil to find forest destruction. Since the 1970s, there has been a seemingly never-ending battle to save Australia's remaining old growth forests. There have been some wins for conservation, but logging in old growth forests continues, at the same time as bush fires resulting from global warming threatens them. The issues here are not just ecological; they are profoundly moral. In my view, we need to use the rhetoric of sin to talk about what is happening. Destruction of remnant old growth forest is sinful and the church needs to say so, as it stands with those of our fellow citizens who have been struggling for years to get the natural world protected.

The same applies to coal mining and to other pollutants. Australia topped the list of coal exporters during 2020, followed by Indonesia, Russia, United States and South Africa. Together these five countries exported 84.1% of all coal sold on international markets during 2020. As a leading contributor to global warming,

Australia bears an enormous moral responsibility. Neither export income, nor supporting jobs in the coal industry can possibly justify this ethically, especially in light of the fact that with government assistance coal-based communities can transition with very little structural adjustment to sustainable industries.[78] The same moral judgment can be passed on much coastal development in Australia, especially that impacting on threatened or endangered species, like koalas.

Drawing on our tradition

The other strength we bring to any discussion of ecological ethics is our long but often neglected tradition of care for the natural world, seeing it as a sacramental image of God's creativity.[79] This tradition reaches back to Saint Irenaeus (c.AD 130-c.200) who reacted against the then-current Gnostic denial and undervaluing of the material world and the human body. His theology emphasised the profound humanity of Jesus and God's intimate involvement in the creation of the cosmos, giving a value to matter that would come to its ultimate consummation when the Lord would come again in the Parousia and in the resurrection all creatures would live in a peaceful and mutually fulfilling co-existence. This notion is picked up by the Roman presbyter and ultimately anti-pope, Novatian (c.200-258). God, he says, gives unity to all creation and He 'leaves nothing empty of Himself. He is always present... penetrating all things'.[80] For Novatian, God and the natural world are intimately interconnected.

This tradition was overshadowed principally by Augustine and the doctrine of original sin, but it still survived in early Irish Christianity. The Irish saints lived in close contact with nature, experiencing, as Richard J. Woods says, 'the world of wildlife, trees, plants and forces of weather, the sea and the vast starry sky as manifestations of God's creative nature, a sacrament of divine presence'.[81] You find this same tradition in medieval saints like Hildegard of Bingen, Francis of Assisi and in the theologies of Thomas Aquinas and his fellow Dominican Meister Eckhart. Saint Francis is, of course, the ultimate reference point for Christianity and the natural world. At the heart of his spirituality was a radical commitment to poverty and humility which overflowed into a passionate devotion to God and a radical love of nature. We see this especially in his love of animals because he saw every creature as a revelation of the nature of God. Like Francis, the Irishman Columbanus (c.543-615) had a similar ability to influence wolves with his serenity. Evelyn Underhill says that the ability to calm agitated animals is common among the mystics because of their access to the profound and primal life-force that, deep down, we share with all creation.[82] Thomas Aquinas understood the cosmos to be a form of revelation, just like biblical revelation, and he picked up Francis' notion of every creature as a revelation of God when he says *Omnia creatura demonstrat personam Patris*, 'every creature shows forth the personality of God the Father... All creatures bear traces of the Trinity'.[83]

In more recent times, this tradition has been developed by in the Catholic understanding by thinkers like Pierre Teilhard de Chardin, Thomas Berry, Matthew Fox, Sean McDonagh, Dennis Edwards, Paul Collins and above all by Pope Francis in *Laudato Si'*. Among the Protestants are the Process theologians Charles Hartshorne, John Cobb and the Australian biologist, Charles Birch, together with the most influential Protestant theologian of the second half of the twentieth century, Jurgen Moltmann, especially in his book, *God in Creation* (1984).

The point here is that, as Catholics and Christians, we already have an established tradition of the centrality of God's revelation in the natural world and a coherent way of speaking about it. We have much to offer our fellow citizens as we work together with them to rescue creation from the ravages of industrialisation, resource exploitation, global warming and biodiversity loss. This is re-enforced by our tradition of social justice and care not just for the human community, but the world community. Ecology gives us a way of relating to our culture.

In a way, all of this provides a context for the PC and a challenge to it. In the final chapter, we'll see how the PC responded.

Part 2
The Actual Plenary

Chapter Six

The Plenary Council

The Plenary: background

At first it looked as though the President of the ACBC, Brisbane Archbishop Mark Coleridge, really did 'get it'. He pushed strongly for the establishment of a PC and he candidly admitted that 'the Royal Commission has made it abundantly clear that... the [Church's] culture has to change, and that bishops and others will have to make bold decisions about the future. There has been a recognition that we [bishops] can no longer put up a sign saying "Business as usual"'.[84] He's repeated the 'no more business as usual' line on several other occasions in the media.

While there's no doubt that Coleridge was the driving force behind the establishment of the PC, he acknowledges that the roots of the decision go back to the early-2000s and to Philip Wilson, the then newly appointed Archbishop of Adelaide. Wilson suggested that a church gathering like a PC take stock of Australian Catholicism and plan for the future. Coleridge admits that 'some bishops were very "toey" about this', but he strongly claims that the bishops were discussing this option *before* Julia Gillard called the RC in November 2012. Nevertheless, he admits that the Commission was a 'huge catalyst' in the decision to use a PC to take stock of the direction of the church.

The other motivating force was Pope Francis as he tried to find new ways for Catholicism, especially by applying his emphasis on what is now called 'synodality'. Coleridge says that his attendance at the Synod on the Family in Rome in October 2015 was a turning point for him. He was particularly impressed by the use of 'discernment' as a process of listening and working toward decision-making. Following his return, the ACBC set up a committee, which Coleridge chaired, to explore the PC option. It reported to the bishops' meeting in May 2016 recommending the setting-up of a Plenary. According to Coleridge the ACBC 'overwhelmingly supported' establishing a PC with only 'about six votes against' the idea.[85] A committee of five bishops chaired by Perth Archbishop Timothy Costelloe, supported by a staff secretariat of four people, was established to run the PC process.

Prior to 2021 the Australian church had held PCs in 1885, 1895, 1905 and 1937. The first three PCs, while influenced by Irish Catholicism, were primarily concerned with the adaptation of the Irish model of church to life to Australia. The 1937 PC was different with its agenda dominated by the then Apostolic Delegate (a papal representative without diplomatic recognition), Archbishop Giovanni Panico, a 'tough and abrasive', but overly anxious Italian, whose English was limited and whose nickname was 'Panicky Jack'![86] Panico, like previous Apostolic Delegates, worked to apply the 1917 *Code of Canon Law* to the local church and to mould Australian Catholicism according to the Vatican model. To achieve this, Panico bullied the indecisive local bishops into accepting his agenda for the 1937 PC. He was also determined to break Irish control of the Australian hierarchy. In 1935, the year he was appointed, there were Irish-born archbishops in Melbourne, Brisbane, Perth, Adelaide and Hobart and in several other dioceses. Panico was particularly determined to unseat Melbourne's Daniel

Mannix.[87] In this he was spectacularly unsuccessful. When he was appointed papal nuncio to Peru in 1948, Mannix still had fifteen more years left to run as Archbishop of Melbourne.

Thirty-two bishops from Australia and New Zealand were present for the early September 1937 Plenary meeting in Sydney, presided over by Panico. Historian of Australian PCs, Peter Wilkinson, says the bishops present 'did little more than read the 685 draft decrees... propose some small modifications, and [then] approve them'. There was no 'substantive debate or open discussion'. The decisions of the previous PCs were swept aside when, as Wilkinson says, 'almost all the laws developed with almost 93 years of synodal effort to suit the local Australian context with its unique culture, climate and vast distances, were abrogated. They were replaced by a Euro-centric *Code of Canon Law*'. All who took part in this PC were sworn to secrecy in perpetuity as to what transpired in the meetings. Wilkinson quotes expert canonist Ian Waters saying that the Australian bishops 'must bear part of the blame' for this. 'The bishops had been urged repeatedly to prepare for a plenary council, but they kept procrastinating. If they had accepted the invitation, firmly taken control, and actively determined the agenda and procedure, [Panico]... would have found it much more difficult to have a Rome-centred and controlled Council'.[88] Clearly the Australian bishops have a long-established habit of abrogating responsibility for the local church and hiding behind 'decisions beyond their control'.

While much of the canon law-inspired 685 decrees focused on intramural issues like liturgy, sacraments, the lives of priests and religious, mixed marriages, the selection of bishops (the Roman emphasis was on appointing Australian-born priests and centralising the appointment power in the hands of the Apostolic Delegate), the decrees also pronounced on trivia like modest dress for women (women's bathing costumes were a constant pre-occupation for the then long-serving Sydney archbishop, Michael Kelly), priests avoiding horse and dog racing and the evils of the cinema. However, the bishops, independent of Panico, issued a joint pastoral letter focusing mainly on Communism but, with the stock market collapse and Depression of the early 1930s fresh in their minds, they spoke about unemployment as 'a serious blot on our social system' and called for 'the fullest measure of justice' for workers, a clear reference to the church's social justice tradition.

The bishops also decided to establish the Australian National Secretariat of Catholic Action. The inspiration for this emerged originally from the Campion Society founded at Melbourne's Central Catholic Library in 1931. The Campions were a group of laymen focused on Catholic social teaching who also founded the *Catholic Worker* newspaper which eventually split off from the more conservative Campions to become increasingly leftist. It was the Campions who provided the nucleus for the National Secretariat of Catholic Action which was strongly promoted by Archbishop Mannix. He encouraged lay initiative and a number of influential organisations emerged from Melbourne in the 1930s: the Young Christian Workers, derived from the movement begun by the Belgian priest, Joseph Cardijn, the National Catholic Rural Movement and the National Catholic Girls' Movement. Mannix appointed two Campion activists, Frank Maher and Bob Santamaria, to run the Catholic Action Secretariat. Lay initiative was very much a Melbourne phenomenon; in Sydney, the laity were more under the control of the clergy, themselves thoroughly under the thumb of the pro-Roman, Norman Thomas Gilroy, described by Brenda Niall as 'pious, sensible, limited' and stubborn, who was archbishop from 1940 to 1971.[89]

The Plenary: Royal Commission

What Panico had succeeded in doing in 1937 was forcing the local church into the Roman mould, and it's this papo-centric, authoritarian, inward-looking church that contemporary Catholicism is trying to move beyond. It's been a long journey of fits and starts since Vatican II's close in 1965 as we endured the leadership of the indecisive Paul VI (1963-1978), the long, hard haul of John Paul II (1978-2005) and 'the reform of the reform' of Benedict XVI (2005-2013). The arrival of Pope Francis seems to have provided a way forward, with the gradual evolution of the still ill-defined and undifferentiated notion of synodality. However, the present PC certainly isn't what Francis means by synodality. It's literally the old canon law-based church pretending to be consultative, while maintaining complete episcopal control.

Perhaps burnt by the experience of 1937, the Australian bishops never returned to the idea of a Plenary until Wilson's suggestion in the early 2000s, but it was the RC that catapulted the bishops into calling the PC. The sexual abuse crisis began to emerge into public consciousness from the early 1990s onward, and by the early 2000s it was clear from media reports that Australia had joined the churches in Ireland, Canada, the US and UK in facing a massive scandal. Gradually a sense grew that the state had to investigate what were, after all, crimes. In 2012-2013, the Victorian Parliamentary Inquiry investigated the handling of child abuse by religious and other organisations in that state. While acknowledging the contribution of churches and volunteers, the Inquiry said that 'It is beyond dispute that some trusted organisations made a deliberate choice not to follow processes for reporting and responding to allegations of criminal child abuse', and that 'there has been a substantial body of credible evidence presented to the Inquiry... by senior representatives of religious bodies, including the Catholic Church, that they had taken steps with the direct objective of concealing wrongdoing'.[90]

After further revelations about particular individuals, dioceses and religious orders, the then Prime Minister, Julia Gillard, announced the establishment of a Royal Commission into Institutional Responses to Child Sexual Abuse on 12 November 2012. The Commissioners were required 'through private sessions and public hearings, to bear witness to the abuse and trauma inflicted on children who suffered sexual abuse in an institutional context'. It was also called to 'identify and focus [its] inquiry and recommendations on systemic issues... [making] recommendations that will provide a just response for people who have been sexually abused and ensure institutions achieve best practice in protecting children in the future'. The Commission sat for almost five years; it presented its Final Report on 5 December 2017. It comprises 17 volumes and includes a total of 189 recommendations. Book two of volume sixteen is devoted entirely to the Catholic Church, covering 925 pages. One valuable service the RC provided for the church was the compilation of statistics. In terms of sexual abuse, it showed that of the 9602 priests, both diocesan and religious, active in ministry between 1950 and 2010, 507 were identified as perpetrators, 7% of the total. Of the 5357 diocesan priests in that period, 344 were identified perpetrators, or 7.9%. Among the 4245 religious order priests, there were 168 perpetrators identified, or 5.6% There were 3666 religious brothers active between 1950 and 2010. Of these, 528 were identified as perpetrators, or 21.8%.[91] Ninety per cent of abuse claims were against priests or male religious.

In his evidence to the Commission explaining how problematic or abusive priests were dealt with in the past in Sydney archdiocese, former Auxiliary-Bishop Geoffrey Robinson described the activities of Monsignor Tom Wallace, parish priest of Darlinghurst. Wallace was Cardinal Gilroy's 'fixer' who worked with the police commissioner to deal with and 'get rid of' offending priests quietly whose crimes, including sexual abuse, had come to the notice of police. Robinson correctly tried to place Wallace's activities in a broader social context. He said that it was accepted then 'that so-called pillars of the community should [not] be held up as morally corrupt, and my understanding was that this applied not solely to Catholic priests; it applied to members of clergy of all denominations... to judges, magistrates, senior politicians, senior public servants, senior police... such cases were handled quietly'. They weren't arrested. 'They were threatened and they were somehow removed... it seemed to be a general policy in Australian society.'[92] This is an important caveat that is often forgotten nowadays. Robinson told the Commission that after his death in 1982 no one replaced Wallace as Sydney archdiocesan fixer and that he didn't know if there were similar 'priest-fixers' in other dioceses. Evidence to the Commission makes it clear that serial abusers were usually dealt with by their bishops or religious superiors who sent them for psychological assessment and treatment, and then often returned them to ministry in places well away from their previous locations. As compulsive recidivists, most abusive clergy simply took their offending with them to another parish.

Bishop Robinson also told the RC that at the November 1987 bishops' meeting, the ACBC held a session on clerical sexual abuse. The presenters, Fathers Brian Lucas, a lawyer and John Usher, a social worker, had studied the problem and Robinson admitted that their information 'was a considerable shock to me, and... to many of the other bishops, because for the first time it showed us that this was a large-scale problem present in most places and in most countries'.[93] Robinson says he became convinced that the church had to respond. He was the key person in developing the *Towards Healing* protocol which shifted the focus of the church's efforts from protecting the abuser and the church, to listening to and responding to the victim's needs.

Robinson's books *Confronting Power and Sex in the Catholic Church* (2007) and *For Christ's Sake End Sexual Abuse in the Catholic Church for Good* (2013) confront the problem head on, but also tackle the root causes by showing that the church's clerical culture is the environment in which sexual abusers are formed.[94] This, of course, tallies with the analysis of Dr Marie Keenan, but it was too much for the ACBC which claimed in early May 2008 that Robinson questioned church authority 'to teach the truth definitively', that he questioned papal infallibility and the nature of the priesthood and, just for good measure, accused him of 'uncertainty about the knowledge and authority of Christ himself'. This, from bishops who had shilly-shallied for years, protecting serial abusers and the reputation and assets of the church, and then had relied on Robinson to do all the hard work establishing the church's response.

Besides Robinson, some seventy-one other witnesses, including lay experts, priests and thirteen bishops were called to give evidence in Case Study 50 on the Catholic Church, which held hearings from 6-27 February 2017. Many of the lay and priest witnesses were honest and informative and their evidence helped the commissioners penetrate the arcane theological and clerical world of Catholicism. In contrast, several of the bishops looked incompetent, out of their depth, seemingly lacking basic emotional intelligence which was reflected in their contorted language which seemed childish in its fawning obsequiousness, as they attempted answering direct, straightforward questions. With little apparent grasp of theological and ecclesiological issues, they failed to address questions on church governance, seminary formation and the impact of celibacy. Their fall-back position was to 'psychologise' abusive behaviour and blame individual 'problem' priests.

In the end, the RC's report on the Catholic Church was devastating, revealing a pervasive element of criminality and cover up that has utterly disfigured Australian Catholicism. It also revealed appalling mistreatment of innocent children and their families, not only by priest perpetrators, but even more by church authorities who attempted to sweep these crimes under the carpet and protect the reputation and assets of the church. However, as was made clear by the more perceptive witnesses, no matter how important the sexual abuse scandal is perceived to be, it is a *symptom* of toxicity, not the root cause of Catholicism's problems. While the scandal has revealed the church's dysfunction, the underlying problems of an outdated, monarchical structure, a sclerotic clerical culture nurtured in seminaries, exclusion of women from leadership roles, inadequate governance, mediocre episcopal leadership and an inability to articulate belief in terms that make contemporary sense, have been brewing for decades, long before the abuse crisis was exposed.

The Plenary: preparations

These are the real challenges facing Australian Catholics, but the canonical structure of the PC makes it an inadequate way of dealing with these deeper, underlying issues. PCs are essentially about legislation governing practical issues in a particular church. Canon law makes it clear that a PC possesses 'the power of governance, especially legislative power... it can decree what seems appropriate for increasing faith, organising common pastoral activity, directing morals... [and] ecclesiastical discipline' in local churches (Canon 445). It's completely under episcopal control. The bishops conference calls the PC, decides on its dates and place of meeting, and 'determines its agenda and the questions to be treated' (Canon 442). Only bishops have a deliberative voice, that is a deciding vote; everyone else has a consultative or advisory vote (Canon 443).

There are other models they could have used. For instance, the Ecclesial Assembly of Latin America and the Caribbean which met in Mexico City from 21-28 November 2021 with 1000 church leaders participating. Of these, 200 were bishops (20%), 200 clergy (20%), 200 religious sisters and brothers (20%) and 400 laypeople (40%). This was the first time that laity were included and the meeting called for a more inclusive and synodal church and increased roles for women and excluded groups, and for the church to take the gospel to the peripheries of society. The assembly drew approximately 100 in-person participants to Mexico City, but also included participation by another 900 people who tuned in virtually.

A model like this would have been far more useful in Australia. By calling a PC, the bishops immediately subjected the whole affair to canon law which guaranteed their control of the process and conclusions. In the wake of the RC, the bishops wouldn't have dared to exclude the laity, but they retained the right to decide which laity would attend and what they could and couldn't discuss. It's not unduly cynical to think that the whole thing was something of a 'set up' from the start. What was really needed was a process leading to a kind of national convocation, or assembly of Catholics, where people could speak their minds in order to articulate the real issues underlying the church's crisis. However, there was no hope that the bishops would allow anything like that to occur.

The first stage was a preparatory, consultative phase focusing around the question, 'What do you think God is asking of us in Australia at this time?' This question is generalised and unfocused, so it is understandable that there were a wide range of responses. Nevertheless, Catholics 'whether devout or disillusioned, fervent or frustrated', seized the opportunity 'to speak... their minds' as PC President, Archbishop Costelloe, commented. It was assumed that by Catholics across the country talking and listening to each other, the voice of the Holy Spirit could be discerned. Catholics responded generously, as they usually do. More than 222,000 participated across the country, with 17,457 written submissions sent in from groups and individuals. By any standard, that is extraordinary. Suggestions from the consultations focused on issues like clerical and ecclesial governance, appointment or election of bishops, the role of women, gender and sexual issues, women's ordination, married priests, consultation of the laity in decision-making and many others. The Melbourne-based organisation, Catholics for Renewal, collated, analysed and sorted by dioceses the five major issues that emerged. These were: (1) greater inclusion of all, especially those overlooked by either church or secular society; (2) greater involvement of the laity including sharing the power of governance; (3) greater role for women; (4) ending compulsory celibacy and allowing priests to marry; (5) the ordination of women.[95]

The PC organisers, meanwhile, tackled the task of distilling and summarising the different responses from the consultation. What was produced were six nondescript 'National Themes for Discernment'. The chosen themes were conversion, prayer, formation, structures, governance and institutions. These nebulous words are vague and frustratingly generalised. They don't encourage practical and hard questions about issues like church structures, governance, clericalism, gender, the power and functions of bishops and priests, ministry, the role and leadership of women, consulting the community before decision-making, or evangelisation in a secular culture, the kind of issues that were highlighted by the preliminary consultation as well as by renewal groups from across Australia in many forums, discussions and writing in the lead-up to the PC.

The PC then set up writing groups with the task of drafting these themes into papers which, in turn, led to a 69-page *Instrumentum laboris* (the working document for the PC) which was released in January 2021 entitled 'Continuing the Journey'. Written by an archbishop, a priest and two laypeople, it was described by Catholics for Renewal as 'a huge disappointment... it is a ground plan for inertia. A tedious, meandering document, it lacks... the frankness, lucidity, and boldness which Australian Catholics were entitled to expect of it'.[96] In mid-June 2021, the actual PC agenda was published but, despite widespread criticism of the vague generalities of the *Instrumentum*, the diffuse and amorphous one page agenda outlined six items and sixteen questions largely focused on generalities and internal church matters that simply ignored the proposals and priorities of the original consultations and written submissions. Given the agenda, it was hard to see how PC members could 'develop concrete proposals to create a more missionary, Christ-centred Church in Australia' as the agenda expressed it. It was further modified by the Vatican before approval was finally given.

The Plenary: the renewal movement

Ever since Vatican II, there have been laypeople and priests who have formed movements and groups trying to implement the Council in Australia. Supported in the past by bishops like Bill Morris, Pat Power, John Heaps, Geoff Robinson and others, many of these groups have come and gone, but, since the late 1990s, there have been active, on-going groups that have tried to maintain a vision of renewed Catholicism through petitions attracting thousands of signatures, conferences, publications, submissions to various enquiries, public meetings, media interviews and maintaining dialogue with the ACBC and individual bishops.

An example of the kind of action taken by renewal groups was in mid-2007 when Catholics Speak Out (CSO), then called Catholics for Ministry, drew-up a petition to the ACBC, asking the bishops to acknowledge that there was a major crisis in ministry within the Australian Church and requesting that practical steps be taken to ordaining suitably qualified married men, returning former priests to ministry, as well as encouraging the discussion of the role of women in ministry and in the authority structures of the Church, including discussing the ordination of women and ministerial training for laity. CSO contacted more than 120 parishes across all dioceses in Australia and asked them to request parishioners to sign the Petition personally.

The response was enormous: 16,746 Catholics, including 168 priests, most of them senior parish priests, physically signed the Petition after Sunday Mass. CSO also set-up a meeting in Melbourne's Camberwell Town Hall which was attended by more than 600 people to explain and support the Petition. Despite the presence of an extremely noisy and disruptive group of young reactionaries, those in attendance supported the Petition overwhelmingly. The only response that 16,746 Mass-going Catholics and 168 priests received came *eight* months later in a brief letter dated 9 May 2008 from the then President of the ACBC, Archbishop Philip Wilson. His response: 'The matters [you] raise in the Petition are of quite diverse doctrinal and disciplinary import. They are also largely beyond our competence as a National Conference of Bishops... Your letter seems to underestimate the challenges to faith which we now confront. It would not, therefore, be appropriate in these circumstances for the ACBC to engage in on-going correspondence with you on these issues'. Essentially, Wilson was telling 16,746 Catholics to get lost because the issues raised were 'beyond' the ACBC's 'competence'. But surely, it's not beyond the competence, let alone the responsibility of Australia's bishops to provide Mass and the sacraments and appropriate pastoral care for the local church?

Along with the enormous work put into the Petition, CSO and Women and the Australian Church (WATAC) facilitated a major research project into understanding the actual situation of Australian parishes. Undertaken by Dr Peter Wilkinson, this became *Catholic Parish Ministry in Australia: Facing Disaster?* published in 2011.[97] Wilkinson has continued wide-ranging research into the local church, especially in preparation for the PC and he now works on the Secretariat of the Plenary.

By the end of 2011, the escalating horror of the child sexual abuse crisis was obvious. Driven by the bishops' failure to address the structural issues that facilitated abuse and their denial and cover-up, and concerned that the church and the faith that had sustained them through life was being 'mishandled and destroyed', several Catholic groups decided to take action themselves. 'Fired by desperation', on 17 December 2011, representatives from Catholics for Ministry and WATAC flew to a meeting in Melbourne hosted by Catholics for Renewal (CFR) and Inclusive Catholics at Saint Francis Church in the city. It was at this meeting that the Australian Catholic Coalition for Church Reform (ACCCR) was launched. Given the failure of the bishops to take the lead, 'the idea of the faithful taking responsibility, leading renewal and speaking out was articulated... We saw the need to build a bridge to the future and we all agreed that if we were to lead, we had to articulate a narrative that pointed to the essence and elements of the Church we all yearned for'. At a meeting in Melbourne in January 2012, a *Call to Renewal Statement* was drafted to articulate that narrative and to underpin ACCCR.[98]

The renewal statement reminded Catholics that 'Jesus inspired his disciples to form a community to proclaim and live the Good News of love, justice, equality, self-giving and hope' and that 'Australian Catholics have a responsibility to act in ways that reflect the values of the Gospel, the vision of Vatican II and the best values of Australian society'. To be true disciples, Catholics must 'reflect Jesus' message of love, justice, equality, peace and forgiveness', be directed by conscience and recapture experiences of 'the mystical and the spiritual'. Authority must be 'used wisely and justly to propagate the teachings of Christ', while respecting the role of the People of God. All Catholics, 'men and women, single and married, [must] minister in a spirit of co-responsibility for the Church', and all must work to influence 'Australian society to be ever more just, compassionate and egalitarian'.

In the years since the formation of ACCCR, more renewal groups have joined, so that by the time of the PC there were 19 member groups, including from New Zealand. In terms of numbers, the groups probably directly represent several thousand people as active members, but they in turn reflect a much larger number of people committed to renewal within Catholicism. Yes, it's true – as some bishops regularly assert – the average age of these people is in the early-seventies, so they'll soon be dead! But this cohort brings an extraordinary experience of life and a long-term commitment to Catholicism. As the Letter to Timothy says, they have 'fought the good fight... they have kept the faith' (2 Timothy 4:7-8). Their tenacity ought not be underestimated.

ACCCR has been extremely active in the lead-up to and during the first session of the PC. Despite the drawbacks of the PC's canonical constraints, the decision was taken early on by ACCCR to participate in the process, so that any critique would come from people inside the tent. An enormous amount of work has been done, including three convocations held on Zoom: the first featured US Sister Joan Chittister OSB, outlining a vision for Catholicism; the second focused on the future of Catholicism and the third on whether the first session of the PC met the hopes and expectations of Catholics. These Zoom sessions had up to 3000 people participating. During the actual week of the first session of the PC, Concerned Catholics Canberra-Goulburn (CCCG) and ACCCR mounted a 'Plenary Tracker' on Zoom, comprising eight three quarters-of-an-hour long sessions reviewing each day and focusing on specific issues. There were 2000 people registered for each of these Zoom sessions. In association with John Garratt Publishing, ACCCR have also published *A Church for All: A Guide to the Australian Plenary Council... and Beyond* and Catholics for Renewal have published *Getting Back on Mission. Reforming our Church Together*.[99] At the same time, Coventry Press published *We Too. The Laity Speaks*, edited by Berise Heasly and John D'Arcy May.[100] In a series of essays by various authors, the book highlights key issues arising from the consultations leading up to the PC, as well as the experiences of Catholics working in a variety of ministries, often struggling against an unco-operative institution.

In a way, these activities are only the tip of the iceberg. Each of the groups making up ACCCR have done enormous work, both locally and nationally.

The Plenary: what happened?

The First General Assembly of the Plenary Council began at 11am on Sunday, 3 October 2021, with the Opening Mass in Saint Mary's Cathedral, Perth. Why Perth? Because the President of the PC is Perth archbishop, Timothy Costelloe. The Mass was preceded by a smoking ceremony by Noongar elders outside the cathedral to drive away bad spirits and cleanse the land, and was followed by an eloquent welcome to country and acknowledgment of the traditional owners by a Noongar woman from the cathedral sanctuary.

In his sermon opening the PC, Costelloe drew on *Lumen Gentium*, the fundamental Vatican II document on the church, telling the congregation and on-line listeners that 'We are... the People of God on pilgrimage towards our heavenly homeland, called to walk together in faith, with courage and hope'. If this ideal seemed a long way from the tragic reality of the contemporary Australian church, then 'much of the work [of the PC]', Costelloe said, 'will need to be done on our knees, metaphorically if not literally', and that to be a 'healing and merciful Church' we need to taste 'the bitter gall of our failings and sins, and then, purified by the Lord, begin to reflect Jesus, the face of the Father's mercy, healing and compassion'. He was brief, but his words struck the right note.

Who was 'called' to attend the PC? All up, 281 people were called as councillors, as attendees were described. Of those, 276 actually attended. A religious sister, two bishops and two priests didn't attend for health reasons. Advised by a canonical committee and a group of 19 *periti* (expert advisors) and a secretariat of 10 people, the work of the PC began after the Perth Mass. The *Periti* group comprised ten priests, three religious sisters, two laywomen and four laymen.

Peter Wilkinson, who acted as an advisor on the PC secretariat, has done a detailed analysis of those called as councillors. He distinguishes those 'who must be called and 'those who can be called'.[101] First among those who must be called are the 39 bishops and auxiliary bishops from Australia's 28 Latin Rite dioceses and five Eastern Rite eparchies, plus the heads of the two ordinariates, the military ordinariate (presently vacant) and the ordinariate of Our Lady of the Southern Cross for convert Anglicans, as well as the regional vicar of Opus Dei. These, plus four elected retired bishops, alone have deliberative voice. However, two bishops, Bill Wright, bishop of Maitland-Newcastle, who recently died, and James Foley, bishop of Cairns, didn't attend because of illness. That meant that of the 276 councillors, only 43 have a deliberative vote. The other 233 councillors have a consultative vote.

Besides bishops, others who must be called are 'vicars general, episcopal vicars, some major superiors of [clerical] religious institutes and societies of apostolic life, rectors of Catholic and ecclesiastical universities, deans of faculties of theology and canon law, and some rectors of major seminaries'.[102] This group made-up 101 councillors, almost all of them priests. Before the 1983 *Code of Canon Law* laypeople, including female religious superiors, couldn't attend PCs. This was changed in 1983 and Wilkinson notes that 'Catholics for Renewal urged the

ACBC to seek a dispensation from [Rome]... to ensure that at least one third of all those called... be women (religious and non-religious)'. This was 'granted by the Holy See... allowing up to 44 additional presbyters and other members of Christ's faithful to be called'. All up, according to Wilkinson's analysis, 41 bishops, one Ordinary, one Regional Vicar, 98 priests, one deacon, 24 religious sisters and four brothers, 66 laywomen and 38 laymen attended the PC. All up, 134 laypeople attended, which is 48.2%, and 142 ced, or 51.8%. The overall gender breakdown was 92 women (33.1%) and 186 men (66.9%).[103]

The backgrounds of those who attended are also important, because it gives you a clue as to the attitudes they brought to the discussion. Certainly, the majority of religious sisters and brothers attending would support Vatican II renewal. This is also true of many of the priests. Doubtless there are ex-officio participants, including bishops and other councillors, who sympathise with the vision of a renewed church. However, there were also some prominent conservatives present who would be determined to hold the line against any so-called 'new church' innovations. Another noteworthy issue is the number of laypeople attending who are directly employed by the church, or who work for para-church organisations.

There was a conscious effort by the PC organisers to give women a prominent place. Good Samaritan Sister Patty Fawkner said: 'Apart from presiding at the daily Eucharist, women were involved in every aspect of the PC journey, as organisers, facilitators, chairs and members. Their contribution was essential'. In her PC intervention, she invited councillors 'to imagine a church which allowed the suppressed feminine to flourish... to be inclusive in our language' and to allow 'women to break open the Word of Scripture and to speak from their experience', in other words, to preach. She also says that the PC reflected a 'diversity of race, role and rite... of age, gender, perspective, spirituality and theology. It was a diversity that enriched and a diversity that challenged in equal measure'.[104] From the opening Mass in Perth onwards, first Nations people were also prominent in the PC's public face and deliberations and there was considerable support for the *Uluru Statement from the Heart*, including from Archbishop Coleridge. 'One very particular outcome I am certainly hoping for', Coleridge said, 'is that the Plenary Council will offer a very clear public endorsement of the *Uluru Statement from the Heart* – I think that would be... powerfully symbolic'.[105]

However, the attitude of the bishops to the PC is more complex. We've already seen that many are concerned that their power and authority will be diminished if governance structures are democratised and the laity given the ability to demand answers. It's probably this threat that persuades many bishops to take a cautious stance toward the PC. Sure, a small number actively support it, and there is also a sizeable group who clearly oppose it, or who, like George Pell, are deeply concerned about where it might lead. Since the initial consultation, most bishops have done little or nothing in their dioceses to promote preparatory discussions among priests and people. Some have doctrinal concerns that the faith is being whittled away and are busy setting limits for topics that can be discussed.

An example of this is Sydney archbishop, Anthony Fisher. In a sermon at a Mass concluding the first PC assembly, he said that the Plenary is 'not a parliament making decrees at will, as if everything were "on the table" or "up for grabs." It's a... gathering [of] Church leaders and some others, for prayer and discernment, to increase faith, revitalise morals, promote discipline and plan common pastoral action'. Commenting on what had actually happened, he said that 'All sorts of things came up this week: some imaginative and wise, some unhelpful even impossible' without mentioning specific issues. However, in a clear reference to the renewal movement, he said that in 'the Parallel Plenary Council conducted in some parts of the media over recent months and days, God has rarely been mentioned, or prayer, sacraments, vocation, holiness, saints, communion with the Church'.[106] Similar views were earlier expressed by Broken Bay bishop, Anthony Randazzo. He said that sometimes, listening to the aspirations of the laity, 'when I hear the cry for "a new Church" it distresses me more than a little. [It]... incites us to throw away what exists. To cast away the Church would be to reject Christ himself and to renounce our faith in Him as the Saviour of the world'.[107] That's stretching a very long bow indeed.

The Plenary: the process

Unfortunately, the PC got caught-up in the Covid-19 pandemic. Its original starting date was delayed by a year to October 2021. With most of the country still in lockdown, most PC members participated on-line in a 'multi-modal' format from their home devices, or through small local hubs. An obvious problem was that participants were totally dependent on the on-line process, preventing well informed individuals and coalitions taking the initiative and leading. Not that I'm saying this was deliberate, but the on-line format gives undue agency to those running the process to limit or even stifle voices they don't want to hear. It also meant that informal encounters and off-the-record conversations that occur in normal physical meetings just didn't occur, and people missed opportunities to see and assess each other's ideas, strengths and weaknesses. If you are not physically present to others, it's hard to form coalitions to influence agendas and outcomes, as would happen in normal person-to-person meetings. As an outsider trying to follow what happened, I was frustrated by the PC process and felt that very little was achieved. However, Sister Patty Fawkner said she 'saw the Spirit working during my Assembly conversations' and she was a participant; I wasn't.[108]

In my view, the problems started with the agenda which essentially marginalised the issues that were highlighted as most important in 17,457 written submissions and the consultation process. Francis Sullivan, a participant as chair of Catholic Social Services Australia and the former CEO of the Truth, Justice and Healing Council, says that 'the agenda was deliberately anodyne' with the result that the week 'was devoid of strategic focus'. He points out that 'the Plenary was not presented with any report on what those submissions contained, nor was it presented with any draft resolutions from the submissions. It can only be assumed that the Bishops Steering Group deemed the submissions to be of insignificant value to the Assembly'.[109] It's not as though anything revolutionary was being proposed in the submissions and consultations. I studied theology throughout Vatican II (1962-1965), was an active priest for 33 years in the post-Vatican II church and have been intimately involved in Catholic renewal for 50 years. Yet here's the PC still debating the same 'old' issues like the role and ministry of women, authority in the church, appointment or election of bishops, governance structures including a lay voice, pastoral councils, moral questions, gender issues and equal acceptance of gay Catholics.

These are the same issues that Catholicism has been debating for five decades and were around long before many of the Plenary councillors were born! I'm not blaming them for their birth date, just highlighting the fact that we're still discussing these issues because John Paul II and Benedict XVI and the bishops appointed by them, supported by small reactionary coteries of clergy and laity, have become past masters at endlessly marginalising the topics that really matter for the future of the church.

We also have the problem that a number of councillors are just beginning the process of understanding the questions facing the church, issues that many of us have been dealing with for most of our lives. Again, acknowledging that they can't be blamed for their birth date, in fact they're ecclesiological tyros, people new to the theology and ministry of the church. It's true that at the beginning of Vatican II most of the bishops had no idea of the renewed theology that came to underpin the Council because they'd left the seminary before Rahner, Schillebeeckx, Congar, Daniélou, Chenu, De Lubac, let alone Teilhard de Chardin, had penetrated priestly training. But the bishops used the experts who were on hand in Rome, attended their lectures and seminars, sought their theological advice and updated themselves. Here another comment of Francis Sullivan is apposite. 'The expert theologians, scripture scholars, canonists and public policy advisors were kept at a distance. It was as though the participants were meant to *start from scratch* (my emphasis)'.[110] One suspects that that is precisely what was intended.

While there were many experienced people inside the PC who tried very hard to shift the discussion to important questions, the organisers – either consciously or unconsciously – used the process to side-step the issues they wanted excluded. One way they did this was by using a much-used word in Catholic circles nowadays, 'discernment'. The idea is derived largely from the spirituality of Saint Ignatius Loyola and the Jesuits to describe a process involving the contemplative weighing up of options, a sifting through the movements of the Spirit in one's life. It involves listening to God, to others and to one's own self in a thoughtful, quiet search for the truth. In theological terms, it's seeking to find the way in which God is leading either an individual or a community.

Another term the Plenary Council used is 'deep listening' which is partly derived from the concept of *Dadirri*, a word from the Ngan'gikurunggurr and Ngen'giwumirri languages from the Daly River in the Northern Territory. Dr Miriam-Rose Ungunmerr explains it as 'tapping into that deep spring that is within us' and it involves 'inner, deep listening and quiet, still awareness... It is something like what you call "contemplation"'. Dr Ungunmerr says 'There is no need to reflect too much and to do a lot of thinking. It is just being aware'.[111] There is no doubt that *Dadirri* is a real gift to Australian spirituality. But it has to be asked if discernment and deep listening were appropriate processes for a large on-line meeting geared to decision-making. Clearly *Dadirri* makes sense in a spiritual retreat, or as a process for a spiritual director or a counsellor, or even a facilitator working with a small group trying to discern a way forward. But it has to be questioned in a meeting of an entire national institution that is caught up in a long-term and massive public crisis attempting to make difficult and contentious decisions within a short, week-long timeframe. The problem is that deep listening and discernment can slow down and eventually totally preclude reaching a conclusion.

I'm not alone in these concerns. While Francis Sullivan admits that 'the "deep listening" process of scripture reflection and sharing in small groups did engender a spirit of collegiality', it was his experience that 'it constrained free flowing discussion and overwhelmed any effective canvassing of the issues confronting the Church. The upshot was a week devoid of strategic focus'.[112]

Combined with the reality that many councillors had limited knowledge and experience of theology, ministry and church renewal, these spiritual processes prevented decision-making, resulting in the PC reaching the end of its first session before a consensus was articulated around major issues, let alone even focusing on some of these issues.

The Plenary: what happened?

So, what actually happened during the first session of the PC? Before answering this question, it should be pointed out that while no code of secrecy was imposed on councillors, the *Code of Conduct* made it clear that what was discussed in the small on-line groups was subject to discretion and that people proposing particular issues should not be publicly identified, a kind of Chatham House rule. It was in the reports back from the small groups that councillors' concerns emerged. From these reports we know that there was certainly a diversity of voices and views. It was also obvious that there were people pushing particular issues that they felt were important for Australian Catholicism's future. The result was a mish-mash, lacking any real coherence. This is also the result of the organisers not providing a focus on specific issues that had emerged from the consultations, and an on-line process that prevented leaders emerging with a vision for the future.

Serious business didn't start until the Monday morning after the opening Mass. From the beginning, it was clear that councillors were feeling their way. It was also clear that those with experience in renewal were unhappy with the way the agenda questions had been distilled – perhaps more accurately 'distorted' – from the national consultation and written submissions. However, right from the start, the role of women in governance, ministry and preaching was front and centre. One whole day (Thursday 7 October) was devoted to those who had been abused and hurt by the church. Francis Sullivan commented that 'Confronting the shameful history of abuse is vital. That history is alive today... Unless the implications of the sex abuse scandal are faced head on, I fear the church will struggle to be identified with anything else in my lifetime'.[113] His words reflect those of the prominent Czech sociologist and priest, Tomáš Halík, who says that clerical abuse is a symptom of a disease of the whole ecclesiastico-clerical system which can only be cured by profound reform.[114]

By the middle of the week, some councillors were feeling increasingly frustrated as they became trapped in minutiae while losing sight of overarching theological themes. It was also clear that the Steering Committee was keeping a tight rein on procedures. Another issue that emerged was the question of formality and titles with the presence of bishops in all of the groups. In addition, a bishop preached at Mass each day which gave them undue influence over councillors.

What did happen was that while there is much that still divides Catholics, new coalitions are beginning to form, people are beginning to talk to each other and – in the words of John Warhurst – 'some silos have been broken down... and the life of the church may be enlivened and may never be the same again'. Warhurst also points out that the process 'did not fully model transparency and accountability' and that ordinary Catholics looking on, as well as some councillors, felt excluded from the process.[115]

At the end of the week, the ACBC Media Blog presented a two-page summary of the final reports of the First Assembly of the PC.[116] While this may be selective and incomplete, it does detail the reports of a number of groups. It leads with one group calling on the PC to acknowledge 'the primacy of ecological conversion, personal and communal', the conversion of the church to environmentalism and the 'explicit adoption' of Pope Francis' *Laudato Si'* action plan. In contrast, another group called for renewal through personal and communal conversion. Another wanted small ecclesial communities based on the early church. There was strong support for the *Uluru Statement from the Heart* and 'the inclusion of Indigenous leaders as partners in decision-making at every level of the church'.

Regarding liturgy, there was a call for formation focused on the sacraments and particularly the Eucharist, while others wanted Catholics to embrace 'the diverse liturgical traditions of the churches', both East and West, as well as recognising 'the cultural gifts of immigrant communities... and acknowledge diversity'. If there was any mention of the sub-standard, some might say 'barbaric' translation of the English liturgy imposed on the Australian church in 2010 by the Vatican, there is no report of it in the ACBC Blog. Another group discussed seminaries and priestly formation. While they said that formation programs must be 'grounded in the community', they also wanted 'solid intellectual, human, pastoral and spiritual formation'. While admitting that some elements of seminary formation 'are problematic', there is no mention of seminaries as seed beds of clericalism. They instead called for 'a renewed focus on vocations' and 'a Year of Prayer for Vocations'.

Governance issues were touched on by a group that said that finance and pastoral councils at the parish level should have a deliberative rather than consultative vote and that this be legislated for in church law. It stressed that authority 'in the Catholic understanding is service rather than power'. One can only hope the bishops were listening carefully to that report!

Linked to this was a call for the *Light from the Southern Cross Report* to be the basis for the Second Session of the PC to develop a more accountable framework for the church. Other groups reported on Catholic education and social services.

While interesting in themselves, most reports lack a broad vision of church and tended to reflect people and groups focused on special issues. As far as can be seen the *Periti* were pretty much ignored, except when Australian theologian at Boston College in Massachusetts, Richard Lennan, was called in on 6 October to give a seven-minute talk on 'The Church as Mission', which was well received. Lennan spoke of what he called 'an integral ecclesiology' and it was precisely this that was lacking at the PC. 'Panoramic answers are hard to formulate', John Warhurst says, 'given the style of the assembly', yet it is precisely these bigger ecclesiological issues that the PC must address. Reflecting on topics that did gain traction, Warhurst predicts that 'on child sexual abuse and safeguarding, the assembly will insist on zero tolerance and enduring repentance and generosity towards survivors'. He says that recognition of First Nations culture and spirituality and ecological conversion will become priorities in the context of the church's relationship to culture. On the role of women in church decision-making, he says there is 'a clear appetite for inclusion, accountability and equality', but that 'women in ordained ministry remains a tough battle'. The need for diocesan and parish councils emerged as a priority. Issues of sexuality and the inclusion of LGBTQI+ Catholics remains on the agenda, although church authorities try hard to avoid these issues. 'Most young Catholics', Warhurst says, 'can't abide church hypocrisy towards the rainbow community'.[117]

A key problem is the PC's processes. Cramming an enormous amount of ill-assembled and undifferentiated material into a week that was slowed to a crawl by the on-line process and the insistence on spiritual exercises led to ill-examined conclusions that in the end had to be handed over to a drafting committee. Even worse was the fact that beyond the original national consultation, all of the preparation for the First Assembly remained a secretive and closed shop, with decisions being taken primarily by bishops, the ACBC, and their appointees. This is no longer acceptable and the PC and bishops are now on trial. Catholics are 'feeling so empowered', Warhurst says, 'that the authorities would try this on again at their peril'.[118] He's right; many Catholics and the renewal movement are waiting in the wings to make sure that previous mistakes by church authorities are not repeated and that the bishops realise they no longer own the church. They must now act with transparency, inclusivity and accountability to the People of God.

The fact is that no concrete proposals emerged from the First Assembly of the PC. Yes, there was an indicative vote, but then the organisers shunted the issues off to a steering committee whose task is to formulate proposals that will be put to a consultative vote in the Second Assembly of PC meeting in July 2022 in Sydney, COVID-19 permitting. In the meantime, the same people are still in charge. The challenge will be for the bishops and their staffs to emerge from their cocoons and realise that they are answerable to God primarily via the Catholic community, the People of God, whose baptism incorporated them into Christ and his body. The consultative vote will be followed by a definitive vote by the bishops. Their decisions will then be sent to the Vatican for review and approval. Pope Francis notwithstanding, it will be non-Australian, bureaucratic hacks in Rome who will really make the final decisions about the future of Australian Catholicism.

Key to what happens in July 2022 is who formulates the final proposals to be put to the Second Assembly. It's complicated, involving three committees: the Steering Committee, the Drafting Committee and the nineteen *Periti*. The steering Committee has four bishop members, a priest, a religious sister, a laywoman, a Jesuit brother and PC Facilitator, Lana Turvey-Collins. The Drafting Committee has two bishops, a priest and two laywomen. Both these committees seem reasonably well-balanced. However, every member of these committees is somehow employed by the church. Only one of them, Sandie Cornish, is the sole lay person with long experience in the renewal of Catholicism, particularly in the social justice ministry. As we've seen, the *Periti* are a mixed bunch. They were a late addition to the PC and their role was never clearly defined. What is clear is that the proposals will be largely formulated by clerics and people employed by the church, with only limited input from laity and sisters.

Their task will be made harder given the diffuse and poorly articulated questions and proposals that emerged in mid-December 2021 in the First Assembly Proposals from Small Groups and Individual Members. These were responses to the sixteen diffuse questions that were discussed by the groups making up the PC. According to PC President Costelloe, the December document 'draws together the proposals that emerged from the small groups that met each day, along with formal proposals submitted by individual Members. As much as possible, what follows retains the original voice of those who spoke, without attempts to produce a harmonised or homogenous account'. Only a really committed optimist would expect that these proposals tackled in any way or form the fundamental issues underlying Australian Catholicism's malaise. It remains to be seen what the combined steering committee derives from this ad hoc process.

Unless the PC tackles the issues facing the Australian church with radical reform, the most it will achieve will be to highlight some important issues, but it will have done nothing to tackle the fundamental challenges facing Catholicism. It will condemn the church to a marginal existence with little or no impact on our society and culture.

Undoubtedly, we live in a *kairos*, a moment of fundamental decision-making when the future of the Catholic faith in this country will be decided. In human terms, the PC certainly doesn't encourage a great deal of optimism. But fortunately, 'the Spirit of life... who raised Jesus from the dead, dwells in us' (Romans 8:10), so our hope and expectation is rooted in the coming of Sophia, the Holy Spirit. 'Hope does not disappoint us', Saint Paul says, 'because God's love has been poured into our hearts through the Holy Spirit that has been given to us' (Romans 5:5). Our reliance then is not on ourselves, but on 'the God of hope who fills us with all joy and peace in believing, so that we may abound in hope by the power of the Holy Spirit' (Romans 15:13).

Endnotes

1. *The Tablet*, 24 September 2020.
2. Response to John Gerson in Bellarmine's *Riposta del Card. Bellarmine a due libretti*, 75-76.
3. Paul Collins, *Absolute Power. How the Pope Became the Most Influential Man in the World*, 2018, 263-265.
4. J. H. Newman, *An Essay on the Development of Christian Doctrine*, 1909 edition, 40.
5. John Warhurst, private correspondence.
6. Wwitch group, private correspondence.
7. F. L Cross, *The Oxford Dictionary of the Christian Church*, 1983 edition, 1242.
8. George Pell, *Prison Journal*, 2021, III. December 5, 2019.
9. Avery Dulles, "Catholicity and Catholicism," *Concordia Theological Quarterly*, 50(1986), 82. See also *The Catholicity of the Church*, Oxford, Clarendon Press, 1985.
10. Ronald Knox, *Enthusiasm: A Chapter in the History of Religion: With Special Reference to the XVII and XVIII Centuries*, Oxford University Press, 1950.
11. Paul Collins, "God and Caesar in Australia" *Australian Book Review*, March, 2018, 40-50. Some statistics updated. *Pearls and Irritations*, 5 March 2018.
12. *America*, 26 February 2019.
13. *Pearls and Irritations*, 3 May 2018.
14. EWTV Network, 27 April 2021.
15. RC, minutes of evidence, 29/2/2016, 16186.
16. *National Catholic Reporter*, 10 November 2021.
17. *Crux*, 8 March 2017.
18. Editorial, *The Swag*, Winter, 2018.
19. Catholics for Renewal Newsletter, 2 September 2018. *Pearls and Irritations*, 22 September 2018.
20. Speech to Catalyst for Renewal, 10 March 2017.
21. www.abc.net.au/religion/articles/2012/11/15/3633611.htm .
22. Marie Keenan, *Child Sexual Abuse and the Catholic Church: Gender, Power, and Organizational Culture*, 2011.
23. John Paul II in *L'Osservatore Romano*, 21 July 1999.

Endnotes

[24] Julian Porteous, *After the Heart of God: The Life and Ministry of Priests at the Beginning of the Third Millennium*, 2009.

[25] Marie Keenan at www.childabuseroyalcommission.gov.au/sites/default/files/IND.0675.001.0001.pdf

[26] *National Catholic Reporter*, 22 October 2018.

[27] Paul Collins, *Mixed Blessings. John Paul II and the Church of the eighties*, 1986.

[28] Karol Wojtyla, *Love and Responsibility*, 1981, 271.

[29] Collins, *Absolute Power*, 225.

[30] *The Atlantic*, January/February, 2004.

[31] *National Catholic Reporter*, 12 May 2016.

[32] Paul Collins, *No set Agenda. Australia's Catholic Church faces an uncertain future*, 1991, 14-15.

[33] *Eureka Street*, 24 January 2018.

[34] ABC Radio National, Religion and Ethics Report, 29 September 2021.

[35] Collins, *Mixed Blessings*, 6, 11, 56-61.

[36] Collins in Berise Heasly and John D'Arcy May (eds), *We Too. The Laity Speaks*, 2020, 241-246.

[37] Francis Oakley, *The Conciliarist Tradition. Constitutionalism in the Catholic Church 1300-1870*, 2003.

[38] Response to John Gerson in Bellarmine's *Riposta del Card. Bellarmine a due libretti*, 75-76.

[39] Collins, *Absolute Power*, 23-57, especially 39-40.

[40] Recommendation 16.7, RC, Final Report, Vol 16(2), 682.

[41] Questionnaire and commentary at www.clericalwhispers.blogspot.com/2011/03/vatican-secrets-selection-of-bishops.html

[42] Jane Anderson, *Innovative Catholicism and the Human Condition*, 2016, 15-20.

[43] ibid.

[44] ibid.

[45] Charles Taylor, *A Secular Age*, 2007, 2.

[46] Paul Collins, *Believers. Does Australian Catholicism have a future?* 2008, 94-95.

[47] National Centre for Pastoral Research, *The Australian Catholic Mass Attendance Report 2016*, Canberra, 2020.

[48] Paul Collins, *Between the Rock and a Hard Place. Being Catholic Today*, 2004, 130.

[49] *First Things*, December, 1994.

[50] *The Guardian*, 1 February 2019.

[51] Jean-François Lyotard, *The Post-Modern Condition*, 1984.

[52] www.brookings.edu/articles/the-risks-to-australias-democracy/

[53] *Crikey*, 28 April 2021.

[54] Singleton, A. et al., *Australia's Generation Z Study. Project Report*, 2019. See also *The Conversation*, September 18, 2018.

55 www.mccrindle.com.au/wp-content/uploads/reports/Future-of-the-Church-in-Australia-Report-2020.pdf and www.mccrindle.com.au/wp-content/uploads/reports/Australias-Changing-Spiritual-Landscape-Report-2021.pdf
56 *The Catholic Leader*, 5 November 2020.
57 www.essentialvision.com.au/trust-in-institutions-16
58 www.essentialvision.com.au/trust-in-institutions-14
59 James McAuley, *Collected Poems*, 1994, 242–243.
60 Paul Collins, *God's Earth. Religion as if matter really mattered*, 1995, 154.
61 David Tracy, *The Analogical Imagination: Christian Theology and the Culture of Pluralism*, 1998.
62 Collins, *Rock*, 80.
63 Father Peter Day introduced me to the word 'industrialisation' in this context.
64 Collins, 'God and Caesar', 42.
65 *Health Matters*, Spring 2016.
66 Marta Sordi, *The Christians and the Roman Empire*, 1983, 3.
67 Ramsey MacMullen, *Christianizing the Roman Empire (AD100-400)*, 1984, 85.
68 Adolph von Harnack, *Mission and Expansion of Christianity in the first Three Centuries*, (1908), Michael Green, *Evangelism in the Early Church* 1970), Rodney Stark, *The Rise of Christianity*, 1997.
69 Tertullian, Apologeticus, 39, 7.
70 Collins in Heasly & May, *We Too*, 245.
71 See endnote 54.
72 www.wearechurchireland.ie/dangerous-synodal-process
73 *Vatican News*, September 29, 2021.
74 Address to European Parliament, Strasbourg, April 16, 2019.
75 Dennis Edwards, *Ecology at the Heart of Faith*, 2006.
76 Collins in Heasly & May, *We Too*, 257-262.
77 *La Croix*, 13 December 2021.
78 Patrick McCarthy, "Transitioning communities dependent on coal mining in NSW," Briefing Paper, NSW Parliamentary Research Service, 1/2021.
79 Paul Collins, *Judgment Day. The Struggle for Life on Earth*, 176-220.
80 Novatian, De trinitate, 2
81 Richard J. Woods, *The spirituality of the Celtic Saints*, 2000, 182-183.
82 Evelyn Underhill, *Mysticism: A Study of the Nature and Development of Man's Spiritual Consciousness*, 1961 reprint, 260.
83 Thomas, *Summa Theologica*, I, Q 45 a 7.
84 *The Courier-Mail*, February 8, 2017.
85 Religion and Ethics Report, ABC Radio National, September 29, 2021.
86 Brenda Niall, *Mannix*, 2015, 229, 249. Brenda Niall, *Mannix*, 2015, 229, 249.
87 Niall, *Mannix*, 241-245.

Endnotes

88 *The Swag* 28/2(2020), 25-28.
89 Niall, *Mannix*, 237.
90 Parliament of Victoria, *Betrayal of trust. Inquiry into the handling of child abuse by religious and other non-government organizations*, November 2013, I, xxvi.
91 RC, Proportion of non-ordained religious and priests who were alleged perpetrators, taking into account duration of ministry – revised – June 2017.
92 RC, minutes of evidence, 24/08/2015, 16015.
93 ibid, 16017-16018.
94 Both published by John Garratt Publishers, Mulgrave, Vic.
95 *Pearls and Irritations*, 26 September 2021.
96 *Pearls and Irritations*, 2 April 2021.
97 Published by Catholics for Ministry and WATAC, 2011. Copy in National Library of Australia.
98 See Call Statement at www.catholicsspeakout.com.au/acccr.html
99 Catholics for Renewal, *Getting Back on Mission. Reforming our Church Together*, 2019.
100 See endnote 33
101 Go to www.catholicsforrenewal.org website, click on "documents", go to no.106.
102 ibid.
103 ibid.
104 *National Outlook - Diocese of Parramatta*, 29 October 2021.
105 *Catholic Leader*, 5 October 2021.
106 *Catholic Weekly*, 10 October 2021.
107 *Catholic Weekly*, 30 September 2019.
108 *National Outlook - Diocese of Parramatta*, 29 October 2021
109 *Eureka Street*, 25 October 2021.
110 ibid.
111 www.miriamrosefoundation.org.au/dadirri/
112 *Eureka Street*, 25 October 2021.
113 Catholic Social Services Australia. Plenary blog, 7 October 2021.
114 *The Tablet*, 2 October 2021.
115 Plenary Insight, Concerned Catholics Canberra-Goulburn, 9 October 2021.
116 ACBC Media Blog, 9 October 2021.
117 *Catholic Voice* (Canberra-Goulburn), 15 October 2021
118 ibid.

Bibliography

Anderson, Jane, *Innovative Catholicism and the Human Condition*, New York & London, Routledge, 2016.

Catholics for Renewal, *Getting Back on Mission. Reforming our Church Together*, Mulgrave, Vic, Garratt Publishing, 2019.

Collins, Paul, *Mixed Blessings. John Paul II and the Church of the eighties*, Ringwood, Vic., Penguin Books, 1986.

_____, *No set Agenda. Australia's Catholic Church faces an uncertain future*, Melbourne, David Lovell, 1991.

_____, *God's Earth. Religion as if matter really mattered*, North Blackburn, Vic., Harper Collins Religious, 1995.

_____, *Between the Rock and a Hard Place. Being Catholic Today*, Sydney, ABC Books, 2004.

_____, *Believers. Does Australian Catholicism have a future?* Sydney, UNSW Press, 2008.

_____, *Judgment Day. The Struggle for Life on Earth*, Maryknoll, NY., Orbis, 2011.

_____, "God and Caesar in Australia" *Australian Book Review*, March, 2018.

_____, *Absolute Power. How the Pope Became the Most Influential Man in the World*, New York, Public Affairs, 2018.

Cross, F. L., *The Oxford Dictionary of the Christian Church*, Oxford University Press, 1983 edition.

Dulles, Avery, *The Catholicity of the Church*, Oxford, Clarendon Press, 1985.

_____, 'Catholicity and Catholicism,' *Concordia Theological Quarterly*, 50(1986), 81-94.

Edwards, Dennis, *Ecology at the Heart of Faith*, Maryknoll, NY., Orbis, 2006.

Green, Michael, *Evangelism in the Early Church*, Grand Rapids, Eerdmans, 1970.

Heasly, Berise and John D'Arcy May (Eds), *We Too. The Laity Speaks*, Bayswater, Vic., Coventry, 2020.

Keenan, Marie, *Child Sexual Abuse and the Catholic Church: Gender, Power, and Organizational Culture*, New York, Oxford University Press, 2011.

Knox, Ronald, *Enthusiasm: A Chapter in the History of Religion: With Special Reference to the XVII and XVIII Centuries*, Oxford University Press, 1950.

Lyotard, Jean-François, *The Post-Modern Condition*, Manchester University Press, Engl. Trans., 1984.

MacMullen, Ramsey, *Christianizing the Roman Empire (AD100-400)*, New Haven, Ct., Yale University Press, 1984.

McAuley, James *Collected Poems*, edited by Leonie Kramer, Sydney, Angus & Robertson, 1994.

National Centre for Pastoral Research, *The Australian Catholic Mass Attendance Report 2016*, Canberra, 2020.

Newman, J. H., *An Essay on the Development of Christian Doctrine*, London, Longmans, Green, 1909 edition.

Niall, Brenda, *Mannix*, Melbourne, Text, 2015.

Oakley, Francis, *The Conciliarist Tradition. Constitutionalism in the Catholic Church 1300-1870*, Oxford, Oxford University Press, 2003.

Pell, George, *Prison Journal*, San Francisco, Ignatius Press, 2021, III, 2019.

Porteous, Julian, *After the Heart of God: The Life and Ministry of Priests at the Beginning of the Third Millennium*, Connor Court Publishing, Ballan, 2009.

Singleton, A et al., *Australia's Generation Z Study. Project Report*, 2019.

Sordi, Marta, *The Christians and the Roman Empire*, London, Groom Helm, Engl. Trans., 1983.

Stark, Rodney, *The Rise of Christianity*, Princeton, Princeton University Press, 1997.

Taylor, Charles, *A Secular Age*, Cambridge Mass., Harvard University Press, 2007.

Tracy, David, *The Analogical Imagination: Christian Theology and the Culture of Pluralism*, New York, Crossroad, 1998.

Underhill, Evelyn, *Mysticism: A Study of the Nature and Development of Man's Spiritual Consciousness*, New York, E.P. Dutton, 1961 reprint.

Index

A

AGZ Study   68-70, 83
Anderson, Jane   55-56
Australian Catholic Bishops Conference (ACBC)   27, 31, 50, 95-96, 101-102, 107-108, 113, 123

B

Bellarmine, Saint Robert   13, 49
Benedict XVI, Pope   14-15, 24, 26, 28, 85, 99, 117
Berry, Thomas   73, 90
bishops   16, 27-31, 57, 114, 123
   appointment of   28-29, 49-50, 52-53, 116
   theology of   27-28
Bätzing, Bishop Georg   12

C

Campion Society   98
Catholic Earthcare   86-87
Catholicism/church
   evangelisation   79-91
   meaning of word   22-23
   medieval church   47-48
   ministries   76-78
   monarchical model   12-13, 15-16, 19, 42-43, 49-51, 53-54, 57, 99, 103
   mutations of   44, 48-49
   New Testament and early church   43-47

people of God model　　12, 15–19, 53–57, 111, 123
　　triumphalism　　11
Catholicism/ministries　　25
Catholicism/practice of in Australia　　11–12, 26, 59–60, 72–78, 82
Chittister, Sister Joan　　110
Clark, Father James　　31
Coleridge, Archbishop Mark　　27, 42, 95–96, 114
Concerned Catholics Canberra-Goulburn (CCCG)　　110
conciliarism　　48
Congregation for Bishops　　28, 49, 52
Cornish, Sandie　　124
Costelloe, Archbishop Timothy　　96, 105, 111, 124
culture, Australian　　21–22, 58, 73, 75

D

Dawkins, Richard　　62–63
discernment, use of at PC　　117–119
Dulles, Cardinal Avery　　23

E

Ecclesial Assembly of Latin America and Caribbean　　104
ecological issues/conversion　　85–86, 121–122
Edwards, Dennis　　86, 90

F

faith practice　　72–74
Fawkner, Sister Patty　　113–114, 116
Fisher, Archbishop Anthony　　114–115
Francis, Pope　　30, 40, 51, 84–85, 87, 96, 99
fundamentalism　　62–63

G

Garrett, Graeme 74
Gillard, Julia, Prime Minister 95, 100
Gilroy, Cardinal Norman Thomas 98, 101
Gratian, monk 48
greed 64–65
Greeley, Father Andrew 39–40
Green, Michael 81
Gregory VII, Pope 48

H

Halík, Father Tomáš 120
Hayne, Justice Kenneth 65
Hodgens, Father Eric 28
Hopkins, Gerard Manley 74
Horan, Father Daniel P. 29–30

I

individualism 56, 63–64, 66, 71
infallibility of pope 13, 49
Innocent III, Pope 48
'Innovative Catholics' 55
Instrumentum laboris 106
Irenaeus, Saint 89

J

John Paul II, Pope 15, 26, 33–36, 50, 85, 99, 117
Judeo-Christians 44–45

K

kairos 40
Keenan, Professor Marie 32–34, 37, 102
Knox, Monsignor Ronald 24

L

Laudato Si' (2015) 85–86, 90, 121
Lennan, Professor Richard 122
LGBTQI
 Catholics 84–85, 116, 122
Light from the Southern Cross Report 50–53
Love and Responsibility (K. Wojtyla) 36
Lyotard, Jean-François 66

M

Mannix, Archbishop Daniel 96–98
McAuley, James 72–73
McCarrick, Theodore 35
McCrindle Research 69–70
McDonagh, Father Sean 90
Moltmann, Professor Jurgen 90
Montanists 80
multiculturalism 68, 70
Mulvaney, Joe 83

N

nature, as sacrament 89–91
'New Atheists' 63
Newman, Saint John Henry 14–15, 51
Nietzsche, Friedrich 66

O

O'Brien, Keith 35
old growth forests 87–88
Olier, Père Jean-Jacques 37–38
Ouellet, Cardinal Marc 28

P

Panico, Archbishop Giovanni 96–97, 99
Pannenberg, Wolfhart 61–62
Parkinson, Professor Patrick 32
Paul VI, Pope 26, 99
Pell, Cardinal George 21, 28–29, 114
Plenary Council
    consultation of Catholics 105–106, 116
    Indigenous participation 111, 114
    membership of 112–114
    online process 115, 119
    periti (experts) 112, 122, 124
    preparations for 95–96, 103, 105–106
    previous plenaries 12, 96–98
    problems with 21, 42, 116–117, 119–120, 122–123
    Second Assembly 123–125, 12, 21, 86, 95, 99, 103–105
Porteous, Archbishop Julian 34
post-modernism 66–67, 73
priests/priesthood
    celibacy 36–39, 103
    foreign 31
    'John Paul II priests' 39
    'ontological change' 33–34, 37
    seminary training 37, 39–40, 52, 103, 121
    theology of 38
    Vatican II generation 27, 40

R

Randazzo, Bishop Anthony 115
religion, Australian views on 68–70
remnant theology 23–24

renewal movements *12, 107, 115*
   ACCCR *109–111*
   Catholics for Ministry/Catholics speak out *52, 107–108*
   WATAC *108*
   Women's Wisdom in the Church (WWitch) *18*
Robinson, Bishop Geoffrey *101–102, 107*
Royal Commission *16, 24, 41, 95, 99–100*
   and Catholic church *100*
Rundle Guy *68*

S
Saint Vincent de Paul Society *25, 76*
schism *18–19*
secularism *58–62*
sexual abuse *24, 32–37, 60, 84, 99–100, 108, 120, 122*
   John Paul II and *33–34*
   psychology of abusers *32–35*
   sexuality *36*
sexuality *35, 38*
social media *61, 64, 66–67*
Society of Saint Sulpice *37–38*
Sordi, Marta *79*
Stark, Rodney *128*
Steinfels, Peter *40*
Sullivan, Francis *32, 41, 116–118, 120*
Sullivan, Susan *77*
synodality *96, 99*

T
Taylor, Charles *59*
Teilhard de Chardin, Pierre *90*
Tertullian *81*

Index

Thunberg, Greta   *71, 86*
Timbs, David   *31*
Tracy, David   *74*
tradition   *11, 13-15, 56-57, 72*
Trent, Council of   *37*
Trump, Donald   *66-67, 88*
Truth, Justice and Healing Council   *32*
Tymieniecka, Dr Anna-Teresa   *36*

U
Underhill, Evelyn   *90*
Ungunmerr, Dr Miriam-Rose   *118*

V
Vatican Council I (1870)   *13, 49*
Vatican Council II (1962-1965)   *14-15, 19, 23, 99, 109, 113, 117*
    Gaudium et Spes   *22, 26*
    Lumen Gentium   *53-54, 111*
viri probati   *30-31*
Von Harnack, Adolph   *80-81*

W
Wall Street (film)   *65*
Wallace, Monsignor Tom   *101*
Warhurst, Emeritus Professor John   *120, 122-123*
Wilkinson, Dr Peter   *97, 108, 112-113*
Wilson, Archbishop Philip   *95, 99, 108*
Women   *85, 103, 107, 113-114, 116*
    in decision making   *120, 122*
    in early church   *43, 45-46, 81*
    loss of by church   *12, 60, 84*
Woods, Richard J   *90*

www.ingramcontent.com/pod-product-compliance
Lightning Source LLC
Chambersburg PA
CBHW011317080526
44588CB00020B/2737

* 9 7 8 1 9 2 2 5 8 9 1 6 3 *